T0078057

Grace like Chocolate Syrup: Good over Everything

CAROL A. JIMERSON

WESTBOW
PRESS®
A DIVISION OF THOMAS NELSON
& ZONDERVAN

Scripture quotations marked (NIV) are taken from the Holy Bible, New International Version®, NIV®. Copyright © 1973, 1978, 1984, 2011 by Biblica, Inc.™ Used by permission of Zondervan. All rights reserved worldwide. www.zondervan.com The "NIV" and "New International Version" are trademarks registered in the United States Patent and Trademark Office by Biblica, Inc.™

Scripture taken from the New King James Version®. Copyright © 1982 by Thomas Nelson. Used by permission. All rights reserved.

Scripture quotations taken from the New American Standard Bible® (NASB), Copyright © 1960, 1962, 1963, 1968, 1971, 1972, 1973, 1975, 1977, 1995 by The Lockman Foundation Used by permission. www.Lockman.org

Scripture quotations marked (ESV) are from the ESV® Bible (The Holy Bible, English Standard Version®), copyright © 2001 by Crossway, a publishing ministry of Good News Publishers. Used by permission. All rights reserved.

Scripture quotations marked (TLB) are taken from The Living Bible copyright © 1971. Used by permission of Tyndale House Publishers, Inc., Carol Stream, Illinois 60188. All rights reserved.

WestBow Press books may be ordered through booksellers or by contacting:

WestBow Press
A Division of Thomas Nelson & Zondervan
1663 Liberty Drive
Bloomington, IN 47403
www.westbowpress.com
1 (866) 928-1240

ISBN: 978-1-5127-7334-7 (sc)
ISBN: 978-1-5127-7336-1 (hc)
ISBN: 978-1-5127-7335-4 (e)

Library of Congress Control Number: 2017901106

Print information available on the last page.

WestBow Press rev. date: 02/07/2017

To all of you who pick this book up and read the inspired words given to me by our God and Savior, and become forever changed from having the abundant life in Christ Jesus that He has promised you. I cannot express the freedom, peace, and joy in living this promise out in everyday life. This promise was made for all of us. You have been given this promise, and I pray and hope you claim and live this promise. Many of Christ's followers need to claim His promise for an abundant and carefree life. In doing so, more people will see what Jesus's promise is all about and want it too.

Foreword

Do you recognize how the everyday experiences of life are often God's call to reflect upon him? I believe you will find this is the premise behind this devotional book. As Carol's former pastor, one of the things I encouraged her—and many others—to do when reading or studying God's word is to walk in the writer's "flip-flops" and experience what they experience. This book is based on her experiences and dare I say your experiences of everyday life. Therefore, to get the most out of this devotional and be doubly blessed for the effort, I invite you to journey with Carol in the coming days and imagine the sights, sounds, and smells Carol shares out of her everyday interaction with God's people and His marvelous creation. Gaze out from her back deck over the misty shrouded hills and valleys surrounding Corning, New York, and picture yourself alongside her as a sister conversing about the spiritual realities of life. See the sunrises and sunsets, imagine the snow and the summer rainstorms, and then ask, "How is God speaking to me in all of this?" Discover for yourself through the eyes of Carol the voice of God for your life. "I have come that they may have life, and have it to the full."

Rev. Charles F. Vollmer, III
United Church of Canastota (UMC), Canastota, New York

Preface

There has to be more to life, church, and Christianity than following a list of written or implied rules. Where is the freedom from all that makes my heart heavy? There must be more than reading my Bible and praying to God whenever I think about it or am guilted into it. Something is missing.

When I asked Jesus into my heart and life I thought I was free to love everyone. Is there something I am not letting Jesus do in my heart? Am I keeping some part of me for me and not for Him? Is that the missing part of life—the one who I allow to take ownership of it? The answer is Jesus having all of me; all of my heart! I do not like not having Jesus own all of my heart. That is when life becomes ordinary and less than what He intended for me. Where can I find that missing part to my deep longing of loving and being loved unconditionally? I can find it in total, complete, full surrender of all of my heart to Jesus.

Frustration sometimes overwhelms us when we watch others have the freedom to love and forgive others, and we seem to have an internal fight over it. Maybe we know and have experienced God's sweet grace poured over us, but then it seems to slip away as we fall back into the way we knew before faith. We begin to believe we have lost our faith, and we believe God's grace has been rescinded. That is the ultimate lie that Satan likes to use when our heart's focus is small and not on the great and mighty power and grace of God. Our minds are weak, and we forget how big Jesus is. We are in constant need of being reminded and encouraged by the grace and unconditional love that can only come from Jesus. When we do not have these encouraging, teaching, uplifting, reproofing and inspired words of God to read or hear every day, our focus on Jesus fades—and the lie seems to appear bigger.

Chocolate syrup poured over almost everything tastes great! That is what God's grace is like when it is poured over everything! Of course, one must "get Jesus" first to receive that great-tasting syrup that makes life sweet. You must get His desire for you to have an abundant life—the sweet chocolate syrup with ingredients full of faith, hope, peace, joy, and love at all times. Have you got Jesus? Are you living every day in His sweet grace and offering it to others? Do you trust Him completely? Are you living His promise of abundant life? Are you grasping and gripping the grace syrup and pouring it over everything?

Acknowledgments

Writers usually begin with an acknowledgment of thanks to those who took part in putting the ballpoint pen in hand to make prose on a page and the inspiration to do so. I too shall make such acknowledgments. The first is my Savior, Jesus Christ, who kept me after I gave Him my eleven-year-old heart that did not know what it meant to have that "blessed assurance." Now I do!

All the people God put into my path have been put there according to His plan that He has for me to be the person He is shaping me to be. Every person who my eyes saw or my ears heard or who spoke to me and I to them was put there by God to help in the shaping me to the person God wants me to be. I am still being shaped after all these years. He put me in a family with five siblings and a dad and mom who took us to church every Sunday unless we had the measles, mumps, or chicken pox. He gave me the mother who He knew would be a key player in shaping my faith—even when I was not watching or willing to be shaped. Deep down, I knew about this faith, but I was not willing to grab it and run with it. Thank you, Mom, for not wavering in your faith and trusting and taking God at His Word and living this daily—right before my foggy eyes. The Holy Spirit cleared the fog! Thank you to my dad who is with his Savior. He answered God's call on his life for a ministry that he only knew a portion of. On the day he met his Savior, I accepted God's call on my life to a ministry He is preparing for me.

God gave me the husband who would help and support me and understand me—or at least attempt to understand me—as my Creator and Savior was shaping me. I believe God gave us both an extra measure of patience and grace. I discovered a passion for writing, and my husband discovered a passion for cooking! Thank you, Kip, for sticking by my side and loving me as only you can—and for picking up the spatula and grill tongs!

God also gave me three children who have had to suffer through my quirkiness as their mom. I won't embarrass them here, but Stewart, Tyler, and Lindsay, you have brought to life the biblical teaching of unconditional love. Thank you. You will always be my children, and I will always be your mom. I thank my sons for looking to God for everything in their lives. They married the women who God handpicked for them; I could not have done such a significant job. Lindsay, you have taught and shown me, in ways no other can, the importance of a simple faith and simple prayer uttered from a heart full of love for God and for others. You truly are a blessing sent from heaven.

All of my siblings helped shape me in some form or another—from getting in trouble together, crying together, laughing together, or letting the Holy Spirit forge a deep spiritual bond between us that can never be broken. Thank you, Sonya Taft, Laura Baker, Jay Roehrig, Linda Deeren, and Karen Miller. You all have had to put up with my preacher practice as a kid to my "princess" attitude when Dad was here and my lack of communication when I was going through my late-in-life college education. I appreciated your patience during those seasons of life.

There are the spiritual leaders who also contributed and sometimes poured themselves with their encouragement, support, experience, prayer, and Christian love into my life with long-lasting mentorships and friendships. For all those sermons I have listened to and allowed the Holy Spirit to apply to my life, I say thank you to Reverend Harry Barrigar, Reverend Charles F. Vollmer III, Reverend Steve McEuen, Reverend Paul Pirano, Pastor Rachael Wilson, Pastor Chris Wilson, Pastor Tom Kuehner, Reverend Jay LaScolea, Reverend Ted Roloson, and so many more pastors who have preached and spoke the truth of God's Word into my life since I was a little girl. A special thank you to the pastor whose first message spoken when he came to my church was a message on the two greatest commandments: your message was music to my soul as the Holy Spirit stirred a new love song in me.

Thank you to my dear friend Tammie Mitchell, second mom to my oldest son, Stewart. You looked after him as he lived at camp during the summer all through his teen years. Thank you for saying yes to using your incredible God-given gift of sketching. Thank you for continuing this project with me even through your roughest moments of life. God bless you and Todd with His utmost riches.

Introduction

Encouragement is something that we are exhorted in 1 Thessalonians 5 to put into practice. God has blessed me with this gift of encouragement and edification and turned my daily life into a daily communion with Him to be shared with others. They are called gifts because we give them away.

I was introduced to social media later in life and really wanted to have a positive outlook on life. Short versions of how God was speaking to me every morning—and its effect His Word had on me—gave me a deeper desire to share so others could also reap the benefits of it. I began to post them on social media websites. This gift increased into various writings on any piece of available paper as I looked around and observed the lives of others throughout my day. I realized how much people need a kind word, a smile, or a nod of acceptance and approval. They need God's love. He revealed to me their needs, hurts, and pains—and their desire to be free from an ordinary life. I began to journal these revelations with the scripture given to me concerning the need. One of the most extraordinary revelations was given to me: the call that God had put on my life. God wanted me! At that time, I was not exactly sure what He wanted me to do or be, but I knew He called me to do things for Him.

During my ministry education, I realized how much I loved to write and express the love that God has for each and every one of us. During these two years, I went deeper into God's Word. Revelations about His great love for me surfaced and spilled out onto the page. I am closest to Him when I am writing about Him and expressing His love for me and mine for Him. The desire to write increases as I commune and write about His love for me.

Best Friends

The Lord's lovingkindnesses indeed never cease, for His
compassions never fail. They are new every morning; great
is Your faithfulness.
—Lamentations 3:22–23

Preschool and kindergarten offer time to play! These years also provide a time of learning and making lifetime friendships. Did one of your best friends in your class or on the playground ever take your crayons, marbles, or jump rope? Did you go home and tell your parents what they did and declare vehemently that you no longer wanted to be friends? Then perhaps you went back to school the next morning and shared your crayons, marbles, or jump rope with the child who took it from you the day before. Maybe you even shared some of your peanut butter and jelly sandwich with him or her because you really liked the child and wanted to be friends. You go through the rest of your school days—and even life—with a true friend who has been with you through all of life's ups and downs and with a heart and mind of grace. You have a best friend for life! Maybe this has even happened recently in the office or at church.

Imagine if Jesus declared to His Father the things that we do when we hurt Him: the cutting words we say to others, gossip, bad attitudes, lustful thoughts, complaining, and lying that we do every day. Imagine if He didn't want to be our friend anymore. What if Jesus' time in the garden of Gethsemane was when He declared these things to his Father? Could Jesus, who was a witness to sin but absent of it, have declared your every known and unknown sin? He knew he would have to possess, bear, and wear them in the presence of His Holy Father in order to make us free from it. Would that not cause us to tell Him how sorry we are for hurting Him and repent of our wrongdoing? Would we ask Him to come back the next day, share with us, and continue to be our friend? Do we want to be His friends?

We know there is no end to Jesus's loving-kindness, mercy, and grace. If there were, He would not have taken our sins to the cross, risen from the dead, or made a place for us with Him. We have a difficult time making room in our hearts and lives for those who have wronged or injured us. We do not show them the loving-kindness, grace, forgiveness, and mercy that our Savior has shown us. He died on the cross for us! He stands by us no matter what. There is nothing he won't do for us. He is faithful, loving, kind, and full of compassion and grace. Those are some really great friend characteristics.

Close friends often begin to resemble each other in their character traits. Our attributes should reflect those of Christ if we are to use his name in ours as Christians. He does not offer us His everlasting loving-kindness or shower us with His unfailing compassion only when we share our crayons with Him. He showers us with the newness of loving-kindness and compassion all of the time. He does not give us what is left from the day before. His gifts are new and full every day. He begins from scratch. There are no stipulations for his faithfulness, loving-kindness, compassion, and grace. These are true Christ-follower characteristics. Jesus just loves—period. That's how He is!

Do You See What I See?

For unto us a Child is born, Unto us a Son is given; And
the government will be upon His shoulder. And His
name will be called Wonderful, Counselor, Mighty God,
Everlasting Father, Prince of Peace.
—Isaiah 9:6

The colorless, pure, radiant, sparkly, faceted snow of a white Christmas sure makes the sloppy, slushy, muddy brown earth beautiful! It covers all the ugliness of the winter and the junk we keep around our homes and makes everything bright, beautiful, and peaceful. We scramble for our cameras to take serene pictures of the pure and spotless fallen snow that is displayed like artwork, untouched by humans, because in moments, the purity is gone. We say, "Ah!" and "Wow!" when we view these pictures all over social media, and then we try to remove the sparkly-turned-sloppy snow from our lives. We break our backs and wreck our bodies while shoveling, blowing, and plowing the pure white stuff out of our way.

What happens when humanity touches the snow? It gets dirty with sand, salt, and pollution—life. Its purity, sparkle, and radiance become ugly. The pictures get flashed all over social media as dirty, negative, sensationalist news that, for some reason, many people are fascinated with. After we have removed it and go on with our lives, we long for another fresh display of the pure, sparkly, white snow to cover up the ugliness again. We long for our minds and hearts to capture the peace, renewal, and hope that are projected by these images of purity. After all, isn't that the greeting found in many of the cards we send out at Christmastime? Maybe that is why we wish for a white Christmas. We wish for the pure, radiant brightness of Christ to come and cover this muddy, sloppy, dying world with hope.

Jesus's hope is for renewed relationships with us. This child, this Son of God, has the whole world on His shoulders. He keeps you and me in his big, strong, tender, gentle hands. He pulls us toward Him so we can become close. He lifts us out of the sloppy, muddy, dingy, formerly pure world. Just as the oppressed Jews of the New Testament under the Roman government were looking for a king to rescue them, we are looking to be rescued from the oppressor who wants us to be slaves to sin. Jesus was and is that king! He longs to be the ruler of our hearts and remove the oppressor—Satan.

Jesus is wonderful! God came to be with us in the flesh as a baby, but He was still the beautiful and glorious God. How wonderful he is! Jesus is our counselor. He gives us counsel through His Word on His great love for us and the plan for redemption and salvation from the oppressor. He is a mighty God. God created the world with His words. He is mighty enough to save the world He created through the birth of His Son, Jesus. He is the everlasting Father. Unlike many of our earthly fathers, God always was, is, and will be there for us. He is the Prince of Peace. In a world where peace is a rare commodity, God sent his only Son. To have peace from knowing that he is able to keep us through all that the world throws our way, we must say yes to Jesus.

Each year at Christmas, our hope is renewed, restored, replenished, and reassured. Why wait for Christmas to wish for hope to come down and cover us? Why not ask for Him today? Without Christ and the hope he brings, we have no Christmas. We celebrate Christmas because it is the birthday of the hope and Savior of the world! I see hope on, around, and from my deck. We can look at the world through the eyes of hope and see the white, pure, radiant, sparkly snow. Happy birthday, Jesus!

Cardinal on a snowy branch

Whirlwinds

When the whirlwind passes by, the wicked is no more,
But the righteous has an everlasting foundation.
—Proverbs 10:25

Storms fascinate me. I love watching them from the safety of my deck. I can watch rain pouring down in the city from the sunny side of my deck. I can gaze at the bolts of lightning traveling through the valleys as the storm travels from west to east. In the winter, I can see the snow squalls following the same pattern. Sometimes the storms travel south to north. As I am enjoying the peace and quiet of my deck, I observe the rain engulfing the hills as it approaches. In the winter, formidable snow squalls swallow the hills on their way to my front yard. I watch them from the warmth and safety of my kitchen.

In the days before a summer thunderstorm, the air becomes hazy. It is difficult to see the rolling hills and beautiful skyline. The sky is not a vivid, sharp blue. It appears to be murky and hazy. The colors of nature appear to be pale and faded. Once the storm passes, all is bright. The view is more brilliant than before the storm. It is like the rain has washed away all the murkiness and haziness from the rolling hills. When I inhale the fragrance of newness and cleanliness that remains after a rainstorm, it is mesmerizing. It would be wonderful and magical if it could be captured and placed in a fragrance bottle. The same can be said about the storms of life that we watch or are a part of.

Our lives get murky and hazy, making it difficult to see beyond the present moment. We cannot truly enjoy its brilliance until the storm passes. When we put our total trust in our Savior to be with us and get us through those storms, life after the storm is glorious. It is glorious because the Savior is always with us—before, during, and after the storm. We can see beyond the murk and haze, which can obscure our sight.

Jesus, who said, "Peace be still" still says this to us in our storms—and to the storms themselves. He wants what is best for us. He knows that storms produce a desire in us to become closer to Him. Who wouldn't want to be closer to the God who loves us in spite of ourselves? He is a firm and everlasting foundation of life, righteousness, salvation, and love.

Life after the storm is glorious, because with Jesus, we have overcome the storm. Our views of our lives and storms are different than before. The haze and murk of the storm are no more as we glimpse the everlasting righteousness of God. He defeated Satan in the death and resurrection of His Son, Jesus. We see life with more vibrant and brilliant colors than before because His glorious righteousness is much greater than our storms. There is no more murkiness or haze to cloud our view of the glorious Father.

If you are watching or are in a storm, know that when it is over, the colors of life will truly be the most beautiful ever. The whirlwind will pass. It may linger for a time, but it will not stay. There is always an end to the storm. The sun will always rise because God created the sun and sustains its rising and setting, and erases the storm clouds so it can shine brilliantly again.

Person watching sandstorm

Maximum Security

He who dwells in the secret place of the Most High shall
abide under the shadow of the Almighty.
—Psalm 91:1

Precious, just precious … what a most inspiring day! Spending some time with God's most precious! Spending time with the really wee ones of the most magnificent of His creation is such a simple yet profound blessing! Oh, yes. There were smiles, bouncing little ones, and a little bit of a natural odor that maybe was not so much a "blessing" to my olfactory organs.

As I walked, danced, and rocked a sweet little one who was fighting so hard to stay awake, I began to think about how much we fight it when our heavenly Father tries to hold us and settle us down into a quiet, peaceful closeness that He longs to have with us. Why do we fight or struggle with His attempts to bring us into that quiet, peaceful closeness?

We think we need to have our focus on the things in this world that hold our constant attention: family, work, church, and friends. We believe it will fall apart if we aren't constantly a part of it or keep watch over it. This gives us a false sense of being in control of the areas we are in constant watch over. We believe that keeping watch over the situations we care most about will bring about our desired results.

Instead of letting God do the watching for us, we do the watching and become consumed by the situation. The situation becomes our focus and it consumes our every waking moment. We think about the resolution, our roles, and the role of others. Consequently, the situation begins controlling us. We may reach the point of exhaustion from trying to keep it all together. We may cry out to Jesus to lift us up in His arms where we can hear and feel the rhythmic beating of His love-filled heart. We begin to settle down and relax. Our eyes slowly begin to close in peaceful, restful sleep as we allow Jesus to hold us, rock us, and whisper His words of love in our ears.

As we begin to rest in the sanctuary of the arms of Jesus, we begin trusting Him to hold it together. It is way better than we can imagine. We begin to realize that Jesus is all we need. Nothing else can provide the protection, grace, peace, and joy that Jesus does. Under His shadow, His pure love for us covers us and protects us. That is where we want to be. We do not want to be released from His strong, loving arms.

We will no longer want to be in the constant watch mode. When He is watching those situations, it is not necessary for us to stand guard over it. The things that once held our hearts captive are no longer as captivating as the secret place—the shadow of the I Am.

The struggle to be free from those arms will end when we trust Him and lean our heads on His chest. Will you listen to His heartbeat and trust Him with all that holds your attention? Will you rest peacefully? Don't fight it. His hands and arms just want to hold you. Rest in His arms. They accept you, embrace you, and love you!

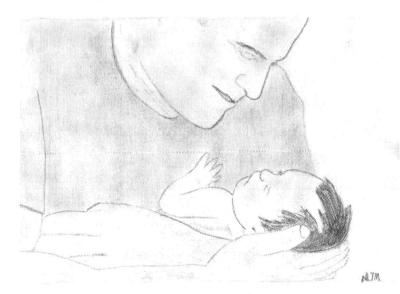

Father holding child

Fast And Slow

So then, my beloved brethren, let every man be swift to
hear, slow to speak, slow to wrath; for the wrath of man
does not produce the righteousness of God.
—James 1:19–20

Hurry up! Be quick about it! It goes zero to sixty in less than four seconds! *Quick, hurry,* and *fast* and other non-slow words seem to be growing quickly in our vernacular. We think that doing things faster is better. We think we need to hurry, be quick, and get things done fast. We think that fast is better—fast Internet, fast food, or a quick trip to the supermarket.

Cars, food, technology, and life seem to be going faster. It's difficult to grasp the speed of today. Fast *is* better when it comes to hearing. We croon over a baby's first words, but in a matter of months, we become irritable parents when their ears do not appear to be working to our liking. We put a lot of effort into teaching them to speak. Do we put as much effort in teaching them to hear? In conversation, it takes a lot of practice and focus to *listen* rather than speak. There is an art to listening. We each have our listening filters. They come from our experiences. When we allow the Holy Spirit to control our lives, He is the filter that all of our listening goes through. He sharpens our listening skills, and He can slow down our tongues.

Without that filter, wrath will come through our speech. God's righteousness in us becomes eclipsed. "For the Lord is righteous, He loves righteousness; His countenance beholds the upright" (Psalm 11:7 NKJV).

We are to seek His righteousness first. What is God's righteousness? How do you produce God's righteousness? He gives us His righteousness—His perfect state of moral perfection. That is totally mind-blowing! What do we do with that? Avoid being wrathful in any and all situations. Wrath and righteousness cannot dwell together. How do others know we are full of wrath? What does wrath produce? If we have wrath inside of us, it will spill off of our tongues in our words and in the tone of our words. We will be swift to speak and slow to hear. Wrath produces unrighteousness, which God does not love. It is not pleasing to Him. It is a fertile ground for sin. It is a place where it can turn to uncontrolled anger. A fruit of the Spirit is self-control.

Wrath is a by-product of lack of self-control. Righteousness is the state of being morally perfect by God's standards to enter heaven. Whoa! Morally perfect? I cannot be that. We cannot be morally perfect by our own standards of following some rules.

Rules are guidelines, boundaries, or standards that God provides for us so that we are reminded of His righteousness. We produce the righteousness of God by seeking Him first—not after our families, our jobs, or our desires. We totally want what He desires for us. How do we know what He desires for us? His desire for us is to live the life He created us for—a life of abundance that is free from the traps of sin and death.

Sin separates us from God and death is the end result. God's desire is for us to be free from sin! Sin is a separator that separates us from the God who is full of love for us. His desire is for us to be in a trusting, loving, and joyful relationship with Him. It begins with faith in Jesus Christ. Faith to believe He died to remove our unrighteousness and give us His. Wow! He wants us to have His righteousness! Who wouldn't want that? Are you filling up your life with by-products of sin or by-products of righteousness?

Slow sign

Junk Wars

Do not store up for yourselves treasures on earth, where
moths and vermin destroy, and where thieves break in and
steal. But store up for yourselves treasures in heaven, where
moths and vermin do not destroy, and where thieves do
not break in and steal. For where your treasure is, there
your heart will be.
—Matthew 6:19–21 (NIV)

Let's face it we have and we hold onto a lot of "treasures" that others may call junk. Most of our homes have at least one "junk drawer." We create reality television shows based on our treasures and junk and our hoarding of it. We pay rent on storage units to store our stuff and are proud about it. More units are being built to store the items we will not part with. We store our belongings between our moves from one house to another. We store our extra stuff, which we can forget is even there because the out-of-sight-out-of-mind mode settles in as we accumulate more stuff. We forget that we already have a blender, a deep fryer, golf clubs, a Christmas tree, and a hand drill.

Instead of obtaining more stuff, why don't we just get rid of what we already have? Better yet—why accumulate it to begin with? Why do we keep all the extra stuff? We may think we can use it someday. When is someday? It is a day that is not on the calendar. Is it a mythical day we made up in our minds so we have an excuse to keep our stuff?

Have you ever been to a junkyard? Have you ever noticed the aroma from our stuff that has been rotting and destroyed by the vermin that make it their home? Varmints and moths have begun to destroy it. What is the cost of keeping thieves and robbers out of our treasures? I am not advocating keeping our homes unsafe from criminals, but we can obsess over our treasures and become fearful of what will happen to our stuff.

We spend every waking moment tending to our stuff instead of living to serve our Savior, Jesus Christ. Imagine all the junk we have stored in our hearts and minds. This life-destroying junk is pain, jealousy, bitterness, unforgiveness, hopelessness, and hatred. It lets Satan break into our hearts, dwell there, and steal our faith, hope, love, peace, joy, forgiveness, self-control, and holiness. When his aroma of sin settles in, we stop noticing his foul odor.

We think we need to tell off that person who hurt our feelings twenty years ago. That leaves the residue of bitterness and unforgiveness, which will eventually reek of hatred. When we are gripping tightly to the pain, bitterness, unforgiveness, and hatred, we cannot grip the hand of God. He can walk us through the desolate, foul-smelling, sin-stench junkyard. We must allow Him to occupy our hearts and minds.

Why not invite Christ to go into the "storage unit" that is holding our "junk" and clean it out? Why not have our sparkly, shiny, heavenly treasures of faith, hope, love, joy, forgiveness, self-control, and holiness in our storage units? Maybe that is why they say, "Cleanliness is next to godliness." What is in your storage unit? Where is your treasure?

Treasure chest

13

The Taste Test

Oh taste and see that the Lord is good;
blessed is the man who trusts in Him!
—Psalm 34:8

Have you ever really thought about what your taste buds are attracted to? Food that looks good? Food we have tasted before? Most likely, we decide not to taste food that it is not appealing to our eyes, does not delight our noses, or has not previously landed on our palates. One cannot possibly know what anything tastes like until we have tasted it. We cannot imagine what something tastes like. We cannot look at something and decide what it tastes like. We cannot smell something and decide what it tastes like. I do not like walking into a home when someone is cooking corned beef and cabbage. The aroma offends my nose, but I like the way it tastes.

On the flipside, I love the aroma of cooking hot sausage with peppers and onions —but my palate says no way! I have recently taken an interest in a television show. The contestants are given baskets of mystery ingredients, and they have to create three-course meals with them. The contestants are judged on their creations by taste, creativity, and presentation. If the plate does not measure up, the contestant gets chopped and must leave the show. If the plate passes the judge's criteria, the contestant moves on to the next round.

How do you get someone to taste your food? Invite them to dinner. You must prepare the food and make it pleasing to the eye. Likewise, we judge God or have an image of who God is depending on how much we "taste" and "see" Him. Taste and sight are needed to find out how good the Lord is. Some of us taste Him with our ears by what others have said about Him. Some of us taste Him with our eyes by what and how we see those who call themselves followers live.

"Distance tasting" is like driving by a restaurant and deciding that we do not like what they are serving. Maybe we look at the menu and decide we do not want this or that. God has invited us to His table. He wants us to taste His Holy Word and His righteousness. Do we accept His invitation? Do we open the Bible and see and taste God?

We only know what we allow our hearts and minds to know about this good God. As we taste the goodness of the Lord, it calls us to want more of Him. We keep going back to His table for seconds and thirds and fourths and more. We allow the tasting to transform us into His likeness: kind, loving, and full of mercy.

Our lives become invitations for others to taste the Lord. Our lives should invite others to enjoy the blessings of what it means to be under His protection. He provides a place where we can be who He has made us to be. Are we creative in attracting others to God? Do our lives present God as a holy and loving God who is always with us? Do we present Him as an unattractive, uncreative, and unpalatable God who people want to chop from their lives?

Many questions of taste and faith can only be found by allowing the "ingredients" to transform our lives by tasting and seeing the goodness of God!

"Oh, put God to the test and see how kind he is! See for yourself the way his mercies shower down on all who trust in him" (Psalm 34:8 TLB).

Picnic basket

15

Do You Understand?

But when I thought how to understand this, it seemed to
me a wearisome task, until I went into the sanctuary of
God; then I discerned their end.
—Psalm 73:16–17 (ESV)

I just can't understand! I just don't get it! Some of us cannot figure out how some people can live that way or with that person or vote that way or think that way. Trying to figure out people is a wearisome task when we compare our thoughts with the actions of others.

Has a lack of understanding of another person caused you to become weary or angry? Trying to figure out what makes other people tick is a never-ending, tiresome, irritating task that we can give up on too soon. I always thought that God did not call us to understand one another but to love one another. He does call us to do that, but that was an incomplete thought. It lacked the knowledge of what scripture tells us concerning His love for us and His command to love others.

Even though He tells us to "love one another" and does not say to "understand one another," there must be some degree of comprehension of each other for us to love as God commands us. I do not believe that loving each other means we have to "figure out" each other. That can cause frustration and unloving attitudes.

The insight we receive from God concerning how we are to understand a person is actually quite simple. It comes from His two greatest commandments: to love Him with all of our hearts, souls, minds, and strength and to love our neighbors as ourselves. When we love Him like that, we will desire to enter His sanctuary and ask Him for understanding, wisdom, and discernment.

When we obey His two commandments because of our love for God, we will be able to appreciate, recognize, empathize, and value each other as God's children. Focusing on ourselves and trying to understand others uses up all of our energy and makes life wearisome. We could use that energy to seek God and love others.

In His presence, we ask for His wisdom. We can open our hearts and minds and put ourselves in their shoes before we open our mouths. We gain wisdom and a better appreciation of others. Our hearts begin to open and soften when we allow God to fill them up with His love.

God's love takes the weariness of loving and understanding others out of the picture. A closed heart gathers no wisdom, understanding, or love for our neighbors. When we are not in the sanctuary of God, we become weary and frustrated by trying to comprehend our differences. We become wearisome when we have a deficit of time in God's sanctuary.

Instead of trying to figure other people out on our own terms, we should try meeting with God. We should enter His presence and sanctuary—the Word of God. In prayer and communion with Him, we will receive wisdom, understanding, grace, and love.

He says, "Come to Me, all who are weary and heavy-laden, and I will give you rest. Take My yoke upon you and learn from Me, for I am gentle and humble in heart, and you will find rest for your souls" (Matthew 11:28–29 NIV).

Maybe that is the key to understanding the gentle and humble yoke that God has for us. It will give us rest from the wearisome task of actually knowing and loving others.

Truth or Consequences

In those days *there was* no king in Israel; everyone did
what was right in his own eyes.
—Judges 21:25

Wow! Everyone "did what was right in his own eyes." Imagine what that would look like today. We would show up to work whenever we wanted to. There would be no need for traffic signs or laws. In fact, there would be no need for laws of any kind. It would be total chaos and destruction. Imagine living in a world like that. We may believe that we do.

Quite a few people only do what is right in their own eyes regardless of the laws or anyone else. In the Israelite's history, the judges could not maintain control over them because they were not accountable to anyone. With the rejection of authority and laws, people developed their own personal laws. Turmoil, chaos, and unruliness rose up. It happens today as it did then. The accountability era seems to be falling by the wayside, and we begin to believe that no one can tell us what to do.

Leaders do not follow the laws they created or voted on. Since no two minds think exactly the same—and everyone believes they are right in what they are doing—we need laws, guidelines, and boundaries that will make us behave the same way. Sometimes we obey the laws we deem necessary to escape the consequences of breaking them.

Do we think about the freedom that comes from obeying the laws? We do not have to scramble to buckle our safety belts when we see the police officer checking vehicles if we are already obeying the law.

"But whoever looks intently into the perfect law that gives freedom, and continues in it—not forgetting what they have heard, but doing it—they will be blessed in what they do" (James 1:25 NIV).

Disobedience of the law brings emotional turmoil. Lies are harder to remember than the truth. Liars can forget what the truth actually was. Remember King David? There are consequences for doing what is right in our own eyes. Children who snatch toys that were taken from their hands end up in time-outs because they did what was right in their own eyes. Almost any child will tell you that fun is not to be had in the time-out chair.

We all want to be right or believe we are right. How many movies and stories show destitute parents trying desperately to feed their families by stealing? Do we bend or completely ignore the rules to rationalize our behaviors?

If we stand for the truth of Christ, we can only win. He is truth! Deep in our souls, we are looking for the truth, but we do not want to follow it. We still have the pride that Adam and Eve had in the garden of Eden. Have we accumulated too much "self" to want to dispose of it and go after truth? Are we blinded to the fact that self brings chaos and truth brings peace and blessings and true freedom?

We say we love God, but are we still doing what is right in our own eyes? Are our lives filled with the consequences of avoiding His truth?

Eye with tear

Garden Party

"For I know the plans I have for you," declares the Lord.
"Plans to prosper you and not to harm you,
plans to give you hope and a future."
—Jeremiah 29:11 (NIV)

I love watching and building flower gardens. The design and careful placement of the stepping-stones pique my interest. Just as an interior designer takes careful study of every detail of designing an interior style that is warm and inviting, the gardener carefully chooses the patterns, colors, fragrance, and shapes of all the plant life and the shapes and placement of each stepping-stone in the garden. The path weaves through the best areas of the garden. We are captivated by its beauty and receive pleasure by walking through it. The gardener may also place the stones in way that has some special meaning. Those walking through the garden will respond as their senses become captivated with all they are taking in.

Outdoor weddings in beautifully designed gardens take careful planning and placement of foliage, flowers, and paths to fully captivate the bride, groom, attendants, and guests. God has put some carefully planned and designed stepping-stones into the garden of our lives. He began placing stepping-stones, fragrances, and vegetation into our gardens before we were born. His purpose and designs are perfect for us.

God placed every leaf, flower, and critter there for us; we have our own gardens. Our garden paths may lead into other gardens and then another and another and back to ours. We could never come close to putting the correct stones in our gardens.

What happens when we do not follow the stepping-stones or paths in our gardens? When we decide to not use the stones that God has placed in our gardens and make our own paths, our feet get muddy or dirty. We may trip and fall, get covered in mud, or bruise a knee or two. We may struggle to get up and get back on the stepping-stones that God has chosen for us.

We may think the pain is too great or we have gotten lost and cannot see the stepping-stones. We may run through our gardens without watching where we are going. If we skip some stepping-stones or stumble over them, we may bruise and scrape up our knees, hands, and hearts.

God picks us up and checks us over for injuries. He applies His grace salve and heals them. He reminds us about the importance of walking on the stones He has placed there for us—and not to run through and skip any of them.

God's stepping-stones are for building us up and keeping us from the things that can harm us. He planned for us to thrive and succeed. He gives us His best. He sees the first stone. He sees the last stone. His stepping-stones are perfect, unique, and carefully placed in the gardens of our lives.

All we need to do is take His hand as He leads us to the next stepping-stone. We can enter the garden with confidence, seek the stepping-stones, and thank Him for the placement of them.

Perfect Imperfection

And when He had removed him, He raised up for them
David as king, to whom also He gave testimony and said,
"I have found David, the *son* of Jesse, a man after My *own*
heart, who will do all My will" … For David, after he had
served his own generation by the will of God, fell asleep,
was buried with his fathers, and saw corruption.
—Acts 13:22, 36

What do you think of first when you hear the name of King David? Do you think of the sins he committed or his great love for God? God chose David to be king over His chosen people, the Israelites. He is one of the most revered Bible characters. He is widely known for the sins he committed when he was king of Israel: lust, adultery, and murder.

We may believe that our sins are lesser or greater than David's. Sin is sin in God's eyes; none is lesser or greater. Why do we remember David's sins more than we remember His love for God? Why do we remember the sins of others more than we remember their love for God? How did he become a "man after God's own heart"? What does that really mean? Maybe we remember the sin more because we lack the belief, knowledge, and acceptance of God's perfect grace.

Our hearts seem bent toward others "getting what they deserve" rather than trusting God's perfect grace. God gave His only Son as the perfect gift of grace. We need to trust for the forgiveness of our sins and trust that He has forgiven others of their sins.

God's heart is full of grace. We must keep our hearts filled with His grace too. David knew God's grace firsthand. When David finally believed and accepted God's grace in his heart, he was "a man after God's own heart who will do God's will." He freely gave the grace to others. When we continue to pour grace syrup on others, we will forget their sins. They are covered by God's grace—just like we are.

The Israelites knew of God's grace. He showered the Israelites with it and led them to the promised land despite their sins against Him. Why are so many people reluctant to share their story of grace? Is it because so many people—even Christians—will remember the sin rather than the grace? Have we become accustomed to being judged by our sins and not our grace? Have we become reluctant to share it?

We should watch and listen to the countless stories of the beauty of God's grace. It will increase our faith and trust in God and encourage us to continue sharing our stories of grace. Who knows what our stories may do for others who are in need of His grace? Sharing God's grace may have some remembering only the sin, but others will see the love and grace of God shining in our hearts.

God forgets our sins when we confess and repent. We should become more like Him. Have you been a recipient of God's perfect grace? Have you given it away freely to others and forgotten their sins? Maybe that is the reason for the lyrics in "Amazing Grace." How *sweet* is the sound? Grace is a sweet story—not a bitter one. Let's remember grace and not the sins. With our sins covered by God's grace—and looking at God's grace in the lives of others—we become men and women after God's own heart. We become full of God's perfect love and grace. We become ready to freely give it to others.

Where God Is

Even though I walk through the valley of the shadow of
death, I will fear no evil, for you are with me; your rod and
your staff, they comfort me.
—Psalm 23:4 ESV

Did you catch the word when in the verse? When "I walk through the valley"; and we will walk through the valleys of life. They include lost jobs, deaths of loved ones, loneliness, homelessness, cancer, addictions, economic turmoil, and suicidal thoughts. We do not walk *in* the valleys; we walk *through* them. We do not remain there.

Walking through haunted houses is only frightening when we are going through them. There are usually creepy, eerie, terrifying, hair-raising, and spine-chilling visuals, and shadows that are harmless. We know they are there—and that we need not be afraid of them—but they scare us anyway.

In the valleys of life, we may know what some of those are. Some may come by surprise, but we still do not have to be afraid. "You are with me!" God is not scared of our valleys! He is there before we are, and when we get there, He is with us through the whole valley. Even when we are out of the valley, He is still with us!

His glorious, shining light turns the valleys of our lives into shadows across our souls. When we are on the mountaintops of life, we do not always see the valleys, but we know they exist. In many valleys, there is a flowing body of water: a creek, a stream, or a river. Have you ever taken a moment to notice the lush vegetation by the river's edge? It brings life to the valley. Many communities develop along the river's edge. Life thrives at the river's edge.

We may have to trek across numerous valleys to get to the next mountaintop. When we do not stop for some refreshing water from the river, the trek across the valley seems to be endless, tough, demanding, and grueling. If we would stop for some refreshment, the valleys might not be so arduous and exhausting.

Do we stop at the river to receive some of the refreshing, thirst-quenching water? Do we avoid the river and try to go across the valley on our own—without water? God places those rivers of life there for us because of His great love for us. He wants us to be amazed by the lush vegetation, be drawn closer to Him, and feel refreshed as we drink from the river of life.

God may use His rod of discipline to bring us to that river for a drink since we may be too stubborn to do so ourselves. When we stop and drink of the river's life-giving, thirst-quenching water, we are revived, refreshed, ready, and able to walk through the valley to the hilltop.

God uses His staff of protection to gently guide us. When you find yourself in the valleys of life, go to the river and drink from the river of life. Jesus is there in your valley. Drink the water that He has supplied for you in your valleys. You will have all you need as He leads you up out of those valleys—each and every time.

The fears and evils in our imaginations are the worst. He douses them with His refreshing water. With Jesus filling us with His life, why should we be afraid of evil? What is there to be afraid of? Whom shall I fear? Evil? Jesus has conquered death and has overcome the evil one!

Action Figures

Above all, taking the shield of faith with which you will be
able to quench all the fiery darts of the wicked one.
—Ephesians 6:16

Diseases in the bloodstream are unseen to the untrained and unaided eye, but we see the effects of diseases on our bodies. Our bodies begin to feel different, and we may feel something is not okay. We go to health specialists and tell them what are bodies are doing. One of the first things they do is order blood tests. They check for impurities that cause our physical bodies to react in unhealthy manners. We cannot see the germs, bacteria, or viruses inside the bloodstream without a microscope.

Once the "bad blood" is labeled, the doctors can decide which treatment will eliminate the virus or germs. Satan's fiery, penetrating, and nonthreatening darts are embodied with diseases. At times, we do not even realize we have been struck with them until it shows up at the core of our being. Our hearts pump our life-giving blood. The "diseased" blood flows throughout our bodies.

How can we prevent the darts that Satan fires at us from penetrating our bodies and allowing the sin disease into our blood? Take the shield of faith and put it in front of those darts. Taking is an action. When we take something, we have possession of it. When we possess the shield of faith, we can prevent Satan's fiery, sin-laden darts of doubt, fear, and selfishness from getting into our blood. All we have to do is use it!

We need to actively and regularly use our shields of faith. Otherwise, we may become inactive and motionless. A body in motion stays in motion. With faith, the more we use it, the stronger and more active it becomes. We hear the word *faith*, and we talk about it, but what is it? How can we grab it and possess it? Faith is the basis for which all unseen things are tested. Faith is a surrender and reliance to the truth. Runners practice running to increase their endurance in running. Christians practice their faith; surrendering their lives to God increases their faith. The more we surrender the more we become reliant on Him and our faith increases. We have faith that God's Word made the world. God said, "Let there be." It was not something we had already seen. When people come to God, they have faith and believe He exists. Otherwise, they wouldn't come to Him. Faith is also necessary to please God. "Without faith, it is impossible to please Him, for he who comes to God must believe that He is, and that He is a rewarder of those who diligently seek Him" (Hebrews 11:6 NKJV).

Pleasing God requires action, motion, or movement. Noah moved with godly fear and built an ark as God instructed. Abraham went out into the desert and dwelt. Sarah, in her old age, received the strength to conceive. In our understanding of life, we must be faithful to Him. That pleases Him. When unseen things are tested, like the shield of faith protecting us from sin darts, will we pass the test as Abraham did? He obeyed God and went to an unfamiliar place where no one knew Him. He followed God's calling. Are we as willing to move as Abraham was? The *Women's Study Bible* says, "Faith is the only essential response to the grace of God."

Will you wield the shield? Will you become one of God's faithful action figures? Let's get moving!

That's What He Does

Sanctify them by Your truth. Your word is truth.
—John 17:17

Speak to all the congregation of the children of Israel, and
say to them: "You shall be holy, for I the Lord your God
am holy."
—Leviticus 19:2

Have you ever thought about whether or not anyone was praying for you? Would you like someone to pray for you? In John 17:6–26, Jesus is praying for you and for me! He prays that we may have the full measure of His joy within us. That joy does not come from a job well done, a giggle from a young child, winning a baseball game, or anything else that we feel happy about. He wants us to have the joy that is deep within. He places it there. Trusting His love for us is unconditional and we are His children is the joy He wants us to experience. He is asking His Father to sanctify us with the truth. He wants us to be made pure and holy—just as He is holy! He does not want our relationship to end with our prayers for forgiveness of our sins.

Jesus wants us to want to be faithful and wholly devoted to Him. Anything less than that would be idolatrous. We go to great lengths to drink pure, filtered water. We do not like to see particles or specks of impurities in our water. We will call companies that specialize in the removal of these impurities or install filtering systems that will remove them. The filters remove even the unseen impurities.

If there is something impure in our lives, Jesus is praying for it to pass through the truth and we can be made sanctified and pure. Jesus is truth. Jesus is the Word. Other gods or leaders of religions do not do this for their followers. The God of heaven and earth wants more for us than just asking Him into our hearts. He wants us to know Him wholly. He wants us to become as holy as He is. We must know God and the character of God.

Many religious leaders have good, insightful, positive things to say to help people have positive energy and become emotionally healthy, but do they help the individual personally achieve those positive thoughts? Do they become more like them? Jesus does! He prays for God to be with us through His Spirit. He wants to help us on our holiness journeys and our quests to become totally devoted, pure, and as holy as He is.

To know just how holy God is, we must study His character. When actors or actresses play famous characters, they meet them or their families so they can portray them accurately. They spend countless hours studying their characters.

We must spend countless hours studying God's character to be able to become pure in word and deed so that every part of our being has gone through the purity filter. We cannot take on the characteristics of God if we do not meet with God and get to know Him through His Word. That is where He tells us about Himself. We strive each day to emulate Him, and Jesus intercedes for us so we will become pure and set apart from our selfish ways.

There is only one example of pure holiness, and it is God. We may see great spiritual leaders like Billy Graham or Dwight Moody who we think are great examples to follow, but God says to be holy as He is holy—not as the Reverend Billy Graham is holy or as anyone else is holy. Jesus is praying for you! Are you willing to get to know God wholly and become like Him?

What Do You Want?

Therefore do not be foolish,
but understand what the Lord's will is.
—Ephesians 5:17 (NIV)

Friends often say, "So where do you want to go to eat? I don't know. Where do you want to go? I don't know. Where do you feel like going?" They list all the restaurants in the city and recite all their menus, but the conversation suspends and rewinds and the original question is asked again. Maybe the destination restaurant should be decided before the invitation is put out there.

Does the dialogue in our lives sound the same way? Do we know where we are heading or what we are doing? We may believe we are living with purpose, but living without knowing God's purpose for life is foolish. If we pray for God's will to be done in our lives, He will show us what that is. It may be different than what we believe—and maybe that is why we sometimes do not pray for God's will. We may end up doing something we decided we do not want to do.

We want to control our plans, our lives, and our destinations. We often miss out on things that would bring us closer to God because we want what we want—even though we know that what we want is not what God wants for us. That means we are letting self be lord of our lives rather than Jesus. We are missing out on the great and perfect plan God has for us. It is planned so intricately and completely that we could never duplicate it.

God knows what is best for us—even better than we know ourselves. Why would we even begin to think our will and way would be better? Doesn't it sound foolish? Why would we not want God's will to be our will? Our wills are foolish and fickle, and they change with the wind. We jump on board with "the next best thing" that the world says we must have or do.

The world is unsteady, but the Lord God never changes. Maybe we do not pray for God's will to be done because we do not know what the will of God is. If we are walking with Him, listening to Him, worshipping Him, and loving Him with all our hearts, minds, souls, and strength, we will know His will.

> And so, dear brothers and sisters, I plead with you to give your bodies to God because of all he has done for you. Let them be a living and holy sacrifice—the kind He will find acceptable. This is truly the way to worship Him. Don't copy the behavior and customs of this world, but let God transform you into a new person by changing the way you think. Then you will learn to know God's will for you, which is good and pleasing and perfect. (Romans 12:1–2 NLT)

As we read God's Word, He tells us what His will is for us. His will is for us to trust Him exclusively for righteousness, happiness, and sin-free lives that are full of grace and peace. His transforming power is matchless.

When we say no to God's will, we are ultimately saying no to righteousness, happiness, and sin-free lives that are full of grace and peace—and His transforming power. God's ways of piecing together something totally magnificent for us is so much grander than anything we could even begin to think of! Do you want to go about foolishly, aimlessly, and undecidedly? Do you want to know what your purpose in life is? Do you want to know what God's will is? Do you want His good and pleasing and perfect will for you?

What Is God Doing?

Are you not from everlasting, O Lord my God, my Holy
One? We shall not die. O Lord, You have appointed them for
judgment; O Rock, You have marked them for correction.
—Habakkuk 1:12

I was my "daddy's little girl." My daddy was the biggest, bestest, larger-than-life daddy who could do everything. He was my everything. I used to believe he was immortal. I believe all children think that about their daddies. He had me giggling almost all the time over the silliest little things. He loved getting me to giggle and be carefree.

As I grew older, the silly carefree life was not as enchanting as it was when I was younger. Other things caught my attention. I wanted to experience new things, which meant I would have to challenge and resist the standard that my daddy had established and wanted for me. After all, he had my protection and best interests in his heart. I, on the other hand, wanted my own way in life.

I did not want to comply with his rules. I wanted my own version of carefree. My version of carefree did not meet the model or pattern that my daddy had raised me with. I had to be brought back into compliance with those standards through various forms of discipline. My selfishness brought heartache for me. In my wayward moments, I was farthest from my daddy. With proper discipline he would lovingly tell me, "This is going to hurt me more than it hurts you."

My daddy wanted me to be safe. When my carefree ways were anything but safe, he had to use the "reproof" rod. I did not like this "fatherly" side of my daddy. I liked the silly, carefree daddy I had grown to love. His love for me had not changed, but I was placing my own desires before the silly and carefree things he knew were best for me.

God's Word shows us His best for us. It is full of promises that He has for us when we do not cross the out-of-bounds marker. In His

Word, He shows us the consequences that take place when we do. He is always on the other side of the out-of-bounds marker to offer us His grace and forgiveness. His admonition, reproof, and warnings direct us back in bounds. If we follow them, we can be silly and carefree and feel close to Him.

We long for the carefree feeling that comes from obedience to our Heavenly Father. We are safest and securest when we remain in bounds. Do we really want God to let us go and be our version of carefree? Does he want us to do whatever our hearts desire at the expense of hurting others—or ourselves? Do we not need some form of discipline or boundaries to keep us—and others—safe and secure in His love?

God has established many "reproof" things to come across our out-of-bounds, step-over-the-line, and spiritually unsafe moments. He teaches and guides us back to His spiritual safety net. At first, we may view them as harsh and unloving—just as a child would say, "You just don't love me. You don't want me to have any fun."

God shows us the bigger picture, and we fall on our knees. We humbly thank and praise Him for those reproofs. Thank you, God, for showing this wayward child Your mercy and grace. Thank you for establishing the many needed reproofs that keep me in bounds and in line with Your ways. Amen!

Jesus holding child

Think about This

Nor is He worshiped with men's hands, as though He
needed anything, since He gives to all life, breath, and
all things … for in Him we live and move and have our
being, as also some of your own poets have said, "For we
are also His offspring."
—Acts 17:25, 28

There is something about sunrises and sunsets that grabs our attention and is mesmerizing. We photograph them and write lengthy descriptive paragraphs and pages about how they have captured our senses and emotions. We anticipate the rise of the sun and watch it drop below the horizon. We hope to see the orange, red, and pinkish hues spreading across the evening sky.

We seldom give much thought to the One who sustains that simple yet complex act of scientific proportions of planetary and cosmos motion. Every evening, the stars are on their appointed courses in the heavens. Who keeps them there? If we look carefully, we can see the sunrise, the sunset, the stars, and all of creation worshipping the Creator!

With the sun rising every morning and setting every evening, the growth of all vegetation and the tiniest insect or creepy-crawly thing doing what they were created to do is a form of worship to the Almighty who created them! I'm not sure if the creation continues or if we are on a continual discovery journey where we discover more of His creations. It is so measureless that we cannot know all His creations in our lifetimes.

There are television shows dedicated to bringing us the newest discoveries from the ocean depths to the highest heavens. God completely created the entire universe and all that is within it—and He sustains it! Everything He created has a specific purpose, and they cannot fulfill that purpose without Him—even the things we do not see as fulfilling a purpose, such as spiders. I wonder why God even bothered to create them. The only purpose I see for them is to terrify me.

We cannot exist without His say so. The laws of physics are actually God's will being done—sustaining His creation! How does creation thank Him for being and doing what they were created to do? Creation worships Him by doing what they were created and willed to do. Nothing He created can be or do without Him!

God created us and gave us breath. He gave us heartbeats, emotions, and feelings. He gave us free will to choose to love Him or reject Him. Have you ever thought about that? Did God just get bigger? Did you begin to realize how much He loves you? He loves you more than any other creation. You are important to Him. He caused your existence to begin with. He loves you.

God created everything because of His will. Life does not just happen. God nourishes and sustains it! The life patterns of all that God created are carried out because of His great love for His creations. When we try to take God out of the picture and consider Him nonexistent, our lives become nonexistent and void of meaning. There is no thrive or drive. If God does not exist, then we were not created. We are nonexistent.

Is your mind boggled? How can I not worship Him? Worship God in faith that He is the I Am! He is the One who gives all life and sustains all life. All of creation declares it!

Misplaced Grace

And all are justified freely by his grace through the
redemption that came by Christ Jesus.
—Romans 3:24 (NIV)

Where did I put that measuring tape? Where are the screws that came
with the some-assembly-required cabinet? I just had them in my hands.
We work on a "some-assembly-required" project and do not get it
completed before we are surprised by some unexpected guests. We
haphazardly put the tools and remaining pieces away in a place we
can easily retrieve them. We may not get back to it for days, weeks, or
months. When we do, we struggle to locate the parts. When we return
to the project, we realize it is missing some parts. Our heads spin as we
try to remember our steps and retrace our actions in hopes of finding
them. We know we have them, but we cannot remember where we put
them.

The search can be overwhelming. The project is delayed until we
decide to get more parts. God gives us His grace for each "project" in
life, and we use it. When a surprise comes knocking on our doors—lost
jobs, death, illness, addiction, or divorce—we scramble to answer the
door. We shove grace in some arbitrary place.

After the surprise has begun to get sorted out, the search for grace
begins. God-given grace sometimes seems to be something we put out
of the way when the surprises of life come to visit us. We should keep
it in hand. How do we keep from misplacing that so undeserved, freely
given grace? When we work hard for something—a new car, a new
house, or a promotion—we tend to take better care of it. When we are
given something, we are more likely to lose it, misplace it, forget about
it, or toss it out with the trash.

Sometimes we shove free things in a closet next to our outdated or
never-worn sweater Grandma knitted when we were seven years old.

God's grace does not have to be worked for or earned. Maybe that is why many of us misplace it or never use it. How do we use and not lose God's grace when unexpected surprises arrive at our doors? We can trust that He sees those surprises at our doors before we do. When we open our doors, He is in the midst of that surprise.

We can use God's grace when we follow His example and His love. We can offer grace to one another by forgiving those who have sinned against us—and not hold their sins against them. We see things being advertised for free and wonder about the catch or hidden costs. With God's grace, there is no catch or hidden cost.

We cannot get grace by working for it. It comes from Jesus Christ! It is yours. Just say a simple thank you once you receive it—and watch what God does in your life! Keep a tight grip on God's grace—and use it to finish your project! Some gifts transform our hearts because of the depth of the love in which they were given. God's grace is transforming!

180

But when the kindness and the love of God our Savior
toward man appeared, not by works of righteousness
which we have done, but according to His mercy He saved
us, through the washing of regeneration and renewing of
the Holy Spirit, whom He poured out on us abundantly
through Jesus Christ our Savior, that having been justified
by His grace we should become heirs according to the
hope of eternal life.
—Titus 3:4–7

Have you ever done anything that you were not proud of? Did it cause guilt or shame? It can become so overwhelming that your whole being is confined and defined by it. Thoughts, manners, actions, and attitudes are swallowed up like Jonah in the whale of guilt or shame.

Guilt and shame, when left untreated, can disintegrate the mind, heart, and soul like acid. When we are in the acidic stomach of guilt and someone shares with us the pure love of Jesus and we accept that love, He causes that whale to spit us out. He washes all the guilt and shame away—and we are new people in Christ Jesus! We are changed for the better. The old self is gone! Never to be a delicatessen for that whale again.

When we see others being freed from the belly of the whale of guilt, what is our first thought? Let's see how long they remain free? Do we watch and wait for the whale to come and swallow them up again? Do we show them God's love, grace, and mercy? Have we forgotten our bondage? Have we forgotten what God's grace and love have done for us?

Maybe the culture around us is so wired to report evil and bad news. It has become so ingrained in our minds that we find it hard to believe people can change for the better. We believe people can change, but most of the time, it is for the worse. We can be skeptics of change. We may define ourselves by our historic actions that will sometimes haunt us.

Satan will use the past to preoccupy us and keep us from showing and sharing God's love with others. This is one of Satan's most used tools. He is the one who gives us the wrong directions on our GPS to keep us off the 180 freeway of change. God's love and mercy recalculates our coordinates for us. Sudden corners, sharp curves, or fallen trees could block our way to route 180. We may have our GPS set to get to 180, but we miss a turn and end up taking the scenic route. Maybe we have not logged and stored route 180 into our GPS.

God will use the obstacles to get us to our destinations. He has already designed and mapped it out for us. We only need to log, store, and trust Him. Trust God for His grace. He has generously given us grace and mercy for our "befores" and our "one times." Trust His recalculations to bring us to the 180 freeway. We may sometimes take the scenic bypass but accept, embrace, and allow His grace and mercy to change us.

If He did it for us, He can do it for others. We must not allow Satan to keep us in the belly of the whale of guilt. That prevents us from believing in changes for the better. Jesus Christ came to the cross freely in obedience to God because of the love He had for His Father. He came so you can get off the unstable route you are on and get on His freeway that will take you home to Him—the One who loves you!

Take a Towel

Jesus, knowing that the Father had given all things
into His hands, and that He had come from God and
was going to God, rose from supper and laid aside His
garments, took a towel and girded Himself. After that, He
poured water into a basin and began to wash the disciples'
feet, and to wipe *them* with the towel with which He was
girded.
—John 13:3–5

Towels are simple everyday items that we have made complicated. There
are kitchen towels, paper towels, guest towels, bathroom towels, beach
towels, tea towels, hand towels, and hair towels. How do I know which
one to use and when to use it?

Towels are generally used for drying and cleaning up, but we have
taken them to a whole new level. Some towels are for display, crafts, or
decoration. Size, fabric, color, absorbency, and intended use must be
considered when purchasing a towel.

Jesus knew the towel He needed. He carried it with Him wherever
He went. He used a service towel. We sometimes leave ours hanging on
a hook or in the closet. He knew what His purpose on earth was for. A
simple towel is a simple act of obedience. Heart knowledge is not head
knowledge. He showed the world that we must know where we come
from and where we are going. We must humble ourselves before we use
a simple serving towel to build the kingdom of God.

What does this simple act of using a service towel mean? It could
mean many things. Doing for the least of these in the community is a
great starting place. Taking a hot meal to a homeless person, a widow,
or people who are incapable of doing it for themselves is one way.
You may see someone struggling with a task and help them. Doing
for others what you would do for yourself and loving others the way

you do yourself opens the door for towel use. It may mean buying extra groceries and delivering them to someone who cannot get out to the store. It may be taking someone to a medical appointment or volunteering to watch someone's children while they grab an hour for themselves. It could mean that you get involved in a messy, undesirable situation at work or at a friend's house. Your Christ-like attitude could change the whole mess into something beautiful for Jesus.

Maybe you go to the one who has hurt you and offer forgiveness and listen to their side of the story. We often forget our towels or do not want to clean up someone else's dirty, grimy, and smelly feet we know will get dirty again. We do not want to get involved in their messy lives and wipe off the dirt and dust and mud with our decorative towels. We do not want to get involved. We believe it could soil our pretty, clean towel.

We may question one another. Why did you let them get dirty again? Why didn't you take precautions so they didn't get dirty again? Jesus wipes our dirty feet every day knowing we will get them dirty again. We must remove our outer clothing of pride that covers our hearts and wrap the towel of humility and service around us.

If you know—with your heart—that you came from God and He has prepared a place for you to return to Him, serving Him by taking a towel and humbly serving others will be priority.

Incognito Jesus

Now when she had said this, she turned around and saw
Jesus standing *there,* and did not know that it was Jesus.
—John 20:14

"Look up in the sky. It's a bird. It's a plane. It's Superman!" Everyone looks as Superman flies through Metropolis. When he is not Superman, he is Superman incognito (Clark Kent). No one seems to notice Superman until someone is in a desperate, holding-onto-life situation and calls out for Superman. That's when all eyes are on him.

Sadly, they only see Superman in rescue mode. They do not see Clark Kent, an average, everyday reporter with a good work ethic and mild manners. Jesus is in our everyday lives, but He is not "everyday" as in average. We can see Him everywhere if we open our hearts and minds and look for Him. We see Jesus in a child's laughter, a stranger saying hello, a smile and kind word from a cashier, a shooting star, the first crocus poking through the snow, or a bird's sweet morning song. Do we see Jesus in the eyes of the homeless, the helpless, and those who are riddled with disease?

If our eyes, hearts, minds, and souls are not seeking Him, we will not be able to see Him in places where we would least expect Him to be—outside of the church's four walls—just like the people in Metropolis did not see Superman without his cape. If we do not recognize Jesus outside of the places our minds have placed Him in, we may be missing out on seeing Jesus in our everyday lives. We expect to see Jesus in a church, a statue, or a painting. We can see Jesus in the friendly hello of an usher or pastor. That is all we see and know.

When we leave the church, we leave our Jesus-sighting glasses there. We do not recognize Him in the little things, the big things, the pretty things, and the not-so-pretty things, the words of others, or our own words and attitudes. Do we see Him in this world? Do we say it is hopeless because we do not see everyone being rescued? I hope we, as followers of Christ, see and recognize Him in awe and wonder of who He is. He is our Savior from sin. Recognize Him in every breath we take, every sight we see, and everyday living, before we get distracted by life that would blind us from seeing Jesus is with us. He is our hope—just as He was the hope for Mary at the empty tomb!

Do we acknowledge Jesus when He calls our names? Do we recognize His voice? Do we call Him *Rabboni, Friend, Savior,* or *Hope of Nations?* I challenge us today to intentionally look for Jesus in our everyday lives. When we see Him, we are transformed by His presence—just as Mary was. When He abides with us and takes, blesses, breaks, and gives us the bread we need to live, may our eyes be open and our hearts yearn to know Him more and more and more. The more we allow Him to abide, the more our eyes and hearts will see the Spirit and be filled with His love. Jesus will no longer be incognito.

Puzzle Logic

"For My thoughts *are* not your thoughts,
Nor *are* your ways My ways," says the Lord.
"For *as* the heavens are higher than the earth,
So are My ways higher than your ways,
And My thoughts than your thoughts."
—Isaiah 55:8–9

Have things happened in your life that caused you to wonder why they happened? What is the purpose? We have a hard time figuring out the logic behind these life-altering circumstances. We may wonder where God is. Does He see and know what I am going through or facing? Yes, He does! His thoughts are for working everything for our good. He knows better than we do. He is righteous, pure, and holy. He can see all the pieces of our lives from beginning to end. He sees all the people and things in our lives at the same time! He is always thinking about you and me!

God knows when to put a piece of the puzzle in place that will benefit the pieces surrounding it, the pieces surrounding those pieces, and the pieces surrounding those pieces. Our thoughts may only be on our circumstances or our situations and how they affect us. We cannot see the piece of the puzzle that God is placing perfectly in place when we are not paying attention to Him. When we are focused on the gazillion pieces of the puzzle of our lives, we cannot see the one piece that He is ready to put into place.

Our circumstances and situations affect our emotions and our hearts and minds. We do not think much about how they affect others. We start to listen to Satan's lie: "For God knows that in the day you eat from it your eyes will be opened, and you will be like God, knowing good and evil" (Genesis 3:5).

Our emotions influence our thoughts and actions, and sometimes we do not control them. We try to put the pieces of the puzzle together, and when we cannot get them to fit, we become hurt and angry at the pieces or at God. We become bitter, and our faith weakens. Even worse, we doubt God's love and the fact that He wants what is best for us.

Human logic cannot see "that in all things God works for the good of those who love Him, who have been called according to his purpose." If we trust and love God completely, we can trust His logic and His purpose for our lives. We will want to dive into the scriptures and prayers. That is where He exposes His thoughts, ways, and logic.

Meditating on those words and keeping them in our hearts will help us understand them. A twenty-minute sermon on Sunday morning or Wednesday evening is not enough for understanding God's Word. Spending time with loved ones reveals many of their thoughts and ways. We can finish their sentences or know what they are planning to do next. We may not be able to finish God's sentences, but we can know Him as He reveals Himself to us through the careful and faithful reading and study of the Bible.

Do you truly want to know God? Are you ready to receive those revelations that He gives you? Are you ready to put your complete trust in Him and in all things that are in your life? He is using it to work for your good and will bring Him glory.

Everybody Wants It

> Rejoice in the Lord always. Again I will say, rejoice! Let
> your gentleness be known to all men. The Lord *is* at hand.
> Be anxious for nothing, but in everything by prayer and
> supplication, with thanksgiving, let your requests be made
> known to God; and the peace of God, which surpasses all
> understanding, will guard your hearts and minds through
> Christ Jesus.
> —Philippians 4:4–7

World peace is associated with the many beauty pageants of yesterday. To have world peace one must have peace within. That peace begins with rejoicing always—not sometimes or when I feel like it. Always rejoice in the Lord. Rejoice, triumph, revel, celebrate, and be glad in knowing that He sees and knows when you really do not feel like you want to rejoice.

With hearts and minds bent toward rejoicing, we can be ready to forgive and look truthfully and honestly toward others when they have wronged us. There will be sweetness in the nature of our character. We pray to God, the One who created the world, and is the only one who can give us the peace we long for. We search for it, but we often reject it because we want it on our terms and with our understanding. What we do not understand, we reject.

Those who are rejected by society; the homeless, the disabled, the deformed and those who do not appear to be like us, we do not understand or want to understand their circumstances or situations. The inability to understand things and people causes us to reject them. We become fearful, irritable, anxious, and unloving toward them.

God does not command us to "understand one another." He tells us to "love one another." Rejoice in the Lord always. Rejoice that He is Lord—and we are not. Rejoice that He is in control. Rejoice that He is Sovereign. Rejoice in knowing that He loves us no matter what we have done or will do. Rejoice that, no matter what is going on in our lives or other's lives—good or bad—the Lord is the same. He does not change. His grace, love, mercy, and righteousness remain the same. They are everlasting. They do not decrease or increase and it is always enough because He is Everlasting. He is sufficient for our ever-changing, fickle lives.

Changes are always on the horizon—even though we prefer and sometimes choose to remain creatures of habit. We look for stability. We take our concerns and worries to God, He wants to hear them. He wants us to know that we can depend on Him and fully trust Him and when we do; His peace will take over our hearts and minds. Through His Son, we will no longer sink and sin under our struggles. We will feel calm in our souls.

Rejoicing in the Lord protects our hearts and minds from the penetrating arrows of evil and sin that surround us. Satan loses! God wants us to know that we can look to Jesus. He is constant, and we can have peace. His perfect peace comes from rejoicing in the Lord because of His constant righteousness and everlasting love.

Reflect on a time when you had a life-changing struggle. How were your heart and mind when rejoicing and prayer were absent? How were your heart and mind when rejoicing and prayer were present? Like a calm pool of water at the end of a rushing stream, peace is attainable through the rushing noise of life. The Lord is the judge, the rewarder, and the righter of wrongs.

Presenting our requests to God, who is Sovereign over all, guards us against the unrest that Satan would love us to have. Rejoice, give thanks, and feel perfect peace. You do not have to be anxious or have unguarded hearts and minds. It is your choice. What do you want?

Dependence Day

I am the vine; you are the branches. If you remain in me
and I in you, you will bear much fruit; apart from me you
can do nothing.
—John 15:5 (NIV)

Being independent is tiring. Have you ever had to move your family and belongings to another city or state without anyone to help you? Have you ever tried moving a heavy object by yourself? Have you ever tried freeing your vehicle that is stuck in a ditch or an icy culvert and it won't budge? Have you ever had a situation that you had no idea how to solve?

Always wanting to figure it out, going it alone, or never asking for help wears us down. Being independent of helpful resources or standing alone on a battlefield can have a devastating outcome. When branches that are loaded down with fruit and break off the tree or vine during a wind storm, they eventually wither and die. The beautiful, delectable fruit turns into a feast for ravenous insects and worms.

Our lives apart from Jesus can be tiring, destructive, and disastrous. After working our minds, our bodies, and our souls into a frenzied state, we may realize that we are unable to figure it out. We cannot do it ourselves—and that is when we finally realize we need help. It becomes a defining moment or a dependence day. We realize that having and using our own resources and strength cannot get the job of life done with complete satisfaction.

All of our money, possessions, relationships, anything temporary cannot give us everlasting joy and satisfy the deep, aching need for Jesus. It is only when we realize that the independence we believe we want, is a tool of Satan. This form of independence keeps us apart from Jesus. Therefore, we can do nothing but work ourselves into a frenzied state.

Dependence day or freedom day comes to us the moment we know in our hearts, souls, and minds that we are nothing without Him and

He is all we need and all we want. Jesus is enough. If we do not break off the Vine during the storms of life—if we go to Jesus before we get worked into a frenzied state over the circumstances of our life—we will produce an overabundance of fruit!

What kinds of fruit will we produce? Will we produce love, joy, and peace? "But the fruit of the Spirit is love, joy, peace, forbearance, kindness, goodness, faithfulness, gentleness and self-control. Against such things there is no law" (Galatians 5:22–23 NIV).

Apart from the Vine, our delectable fruit turns into the rottenness of the flesh.

> The acts of the flesh are obvious: sexual immorality, impurity and debauchery; idolatry and witchcraft; hatred, discord, jealousy, fits of rage, selfish ambition, dissensions, factions and envy; drunkenness, orgies, and the like. I warn you, as I did before, that those who live like this will not inherit the kingdom of God. (Galatians 5:19–24 NIV)

When I think independently from Christ, with my own strength and try to fix every problem that comes my way—or everybody else's problems that get put into my path—I feel defeated and worn. The stress wreaks havoc on my mind, body, and soul (my branch), will break off from the Vine. I cannot see the light at the end of the tunnel until I see Him, want Him first and keep Him first. Is Jesus enough for you? Dependence day is the real day of freedom! Have you celebrated Dependence Day? It will be worth celebrating!

The Way He Looks At You

But the Lord said to Samuel, "Do not look at his
appearance or at his physical stature, because I have
refused him." For *the Lord does* not *see* as man sees; for
man looks at the outward appearance, but the Lord looks
at the heart.
—1 Samuel 16:7

We are almost totally consumed by how others see us. The marketplace is flooded with ways to make us look and feel gorgeous from head to toe. Why do we care? Why do we take such great measures to get others to look at us? What are the measures do we take to get them to look at us?

After taking all the painstaking measures to look and feel good on the outside, we may feel pretty good for a while. When that feeling diminishes, we try to keep up appearances to keep the attention we long for. That can take all the time, energy, and money we have.

Walk down Main Street USA and notice the number of salons. Each salon for hair or nails has its flair that is geared to attract a particular clientele. When I was growing up, I did not know about these salons. My mom wore rollers in her hair to have the wave or curl look, and she was the most beautiful mom. How could one work in the vegetable garden and raise a slew of snotty-nosed kids with constant cuts and bruises that her most beautiful unmanicured nails soothed?

My feet would have given the disciples' feet a run for their "sandals." I did not wear shoes; my feet were planted in the grass and mountains of dirt while I was growing up. Today, we cannot bare our feet unless we have perfect pedicures. We make monthly trips to make our hands, feet, and hair gorgeous. I am not saying that we should not look good on the outside, but when it consumes us to the point where we neglect to look good on the inside, we need to stop and realize what Jesus, who is our greatest admirer, is looking at when He sees us.

Do our hearts look gorgeous to Jesus? You have captivated Jesus's attention forever. He loves you for you. He loves everything about you—no matter what you look like. He loves you if you are short, tall, thin, or fat. He loves your wrinkles and flaws. He doesn't look at hair color, skin color, lip color, or nail color. He doesn't measure you to see if you are the perfect height or weight because His Father created you at that height and weight, and His creation is perfect. He looks deep into your soul and sees that you were created in the image of His Father. You are perfect. The problem is we have allowed the dirt of the world to get rubbed in on our hearts. The fickle wind infiltrates our minds, which makes for an inside that is not very pleasing to the eye. We must go to the "heart salon" more often than the hair or nail salon. The Master "heart styler" sees our unkempt hearts. As we kneel or sit at His feet, He tends to our hearts. He makes us gorgeous to Him and to the world we live in.

Our bodies need to be cared for properly to maintain good health. He is the one who gives us life, but our focus needs to be on the Giver of Life, Jesus, and not on outward appearances. Do we go often enough to the heart salon?

Whose attention is your heart captivating? Instead of focusing on outward makeovers, maybe we should pick up the Bible and focus on an inward transformation that will show the ultimate beauty of the Lord!

Lindsay getting makeup for wedding

Junk Mail

Let your light so shine before men, that they may see your
good works and glorify your Father in heaven.
—Matthew 5:16

No matter what you do to try to stop junk mail, it seems you can never get rid of it. As a letter carrier for the United States Postal Service, I know many statistics, comments, and jokes about junk mail. People do not like all the junk mail that overflows their mailboxes as they must retrieve it, collect it, and dispose of it in a proper manner. The amount of junk mail found in the mail box is a frequent complaint. Since advertisers have paid the postage, it must be delivered. Junk mail isn't free. The sender pays a fee for the USPS to deliver advertisements. Since the advent of the World Wide Web, first-class mail has drastically been reduced—and so has junk mail. Junk mail will eventually find your address—whether it is physical or digital.

Personal junk mail—actions, attitudes, and words—will eventually reach and overflow the spiritual mailbox of others. Even though it is their responsibility to dispose of the junk mail they receive, it is our responsibility to make sure our junk does not make it to their inboxes or social media accounts. We are responsible for what we deliver, including unkind words, sour and critical attitudes, and unloving actions. We should sort and dispose of them before they leave our offices.

Are we delivering more junk? Is it similar to what the world delivers? Is our junk glorifying our Father in heaven? Can't we get rid of unloving actions, attitudes, and words? Yes, we can! We must desire and allow the gift of the Holy Spirit to rework the processes inside us so the junk mail is properly disposed of before we decide to deliver it to those around us.

Have you ever wondered if others even want our junk mail? Do you want the junk mail of others? Others do not want it, and Jesus Christ does not like it when we deliver it to His family. Have you ever considered the cost of the junk we deliver? We may deliver it freely, but there is a cost involved. It could be an eternal expense—to us and the one on the receiving end.

The junk we are delivering may dim our lights, or put out our lights. Our junk may keep others from seeing Jesus and glorifying Him. Just imagine how much more glory Jesus would receive if our lights were shining brightly! Our good works would not be undone when we throw away our junk.

The junk that we deliver remains in the mailboxes or inboxes of others. They may become so overwhelmed that it does not end up in the trash even if we believe it will. What do you do with junk mail? Some people are hoarders and do not have any place for anything else. Eventually they cannot be reached because a fortress of junk mail surrounds them. Nobody waits at the doorstep to receive junk mail, but if we deliver the truth of the love of Jesus to others, they will watch and wait for His love on their doorsteps.

Suddenly

And an angel of the Lord suddenly stood before them, and
the glory of the Lord shone around them; and they were
terribly frightened. But the angel said to them, "Do not
be afraid; for behold, I bring you good news of great joy
which will be for all the people."
—Luke 2:9–10 (NASB)

The sun is shining brightly. There is absolutely no stress or strife. All is calm, and all is bright! The glory of the Lord is all around in His creation! You are receiving one blessing after another. You are receiving blessings from others via your loving and giving.

Life is one big bowl of pit-less cherries! What more could one ask for? Nothing is standing between you and God—or is there? Then suddenly, change has appeared on your quiet blessed doorstep and you become terribly frightened of the change. The quiet and tranquility has left your home, and your life is forever changed! Any number of incidents in life stems from a fallen world of sin and causes the sudden life change. It may be a change in a health, a divorce or other drastic relationship change, or a betrayal of some sort. Maybe it is a new job, a new relationship, or new baby, a new house or home, or a new relationship with Jesus—anything that is suddenly different.

What happens when there is an unexpected change in life? We fear. We wonder what is going to happen next and why things happened the way they did. We replay scenarios in our minds and become frustrated, stressed, angry, or bitter. We do not know how to sort it all out in a way that our minds can manage or understand. Our lives are on a different and unfamiliar road.

These life-altering "suddenlys" can be overwhelming. We struggle with the change that a "suddenly" brings because we are comfortable in the familiar. We think more about the changes and the affect they may have on our lives. Our thoughts can overwhelm us and scare us. Suddenlys do not come without angels of the Lord speaking to us in a soothing manner. They quiet our scrambled, confused and fear-laden minds.

God has promised to bring us the Good News, which brings us great joy! God is not a God of confusion and fear. When God says, "Do not be afraid," He might be saying, "There will be a change coming. It is for your good and My glory. I want you to move closer to me. Without change, you would not move closer to Me. I want you right by My side—closer than you have ever been. Things in life change. They don't always stay the same, but I am the same. I am God—Creator of all, Creator of the universe—and I know all about change. I am in your change, and I have authority over your change. Once you accept this change, you will be praising Me for it. You will see the benefits of it. You will be closer to Me, the struggle will cease, and My peace will be given to you."

Have you ever thought about wanting to be closer to God and the things that prevent you from being there? Suddenlys can produce great joy if we accept them without fear and move closer to God! God's faithful promise of the Good News is that He is with us and brings us His everlasting joy and peace. We have a choice!

Rescued

Then I heard a loud voice saying in heaven, "Now
salvation, and strength, and the kingdom of our God,
and the power of His Christ have come, for the accuser of
our brethren, who accused them before our God day and
night, has been cast down."
—Revelation 12:10

I was an avid watcher of Saturday morning cartoons! I could not wait to see how a fast-moving bird would outwit the clever coyote or how a sweet little bird would get the kitty in trouble. I also liked watching a team of teens solve mysteries as they unmask villains and made the world safe once again. Some cartoons were simple enough: good guy versus bad guy.

I was always in front of the TV. The old style TV; when I wanted to change the channel and go from the prehistoric age to the space age, I had to get off the couch to turn the dial. In one show, the villain began terrifying all the people in the world. He tried to get them to do bad things. He shot arrows and fiery rocks at people to try to get them to do bad things. The good guy supplied rock and fire resistant shields. He grabbed the bad guy and swung him around and threw him off the earth. The bad guy was never heard from again! The people cheered loudly and ran straight to their rescuer!

God promises us that He will hurl the evil accuser down forever. The power of His kingdom will stand. Nothing will stand against it. God's salvation—through Jesus Christ, the Messiah—has come! Through His shed blood on the cross for our sins, we are completely free from sin. We are completely free of Satan's false accusations. All authority through the resurrection of Jesus Christ has been given to us! The chains of sin are gone forever! We no longer stand before God accused of sin. We are free to sin no more!

Satan wants us to feel like we are not free, that we can never be free, that we are helpless and hopeless, that we can do nothing, and that God's power will not protect us from Satan's evil schemes. He is constantly pointing his accusing finger at us and telling us about our sins.

Jesus has overcome all of Satan's methods for our destruction, and He hands us the shield of faith. When we grasp it and hold it out in front of us, it obliterates all the accusations, wrongs, and sins that Satan throws at us to try to defeat us.

Jesus freed us from our sins when He died on the cross. He left them in the grave and conquered sin and death for us! We do not have to let sin have power over us! We can grab the faith-filled shield Jesus holds with us. We watch our Savior throw Satan into the fiery pit of dark anguish and torture. The evil villain will never be heard from again!

Jesus has overcome! God has won! We cheer and praise God as we run to Him and shout glory to Him!

No Swimming

And we know that in all things God works for the good of
those who love him,
who have been called according to his purpose.
—Romans 8:28 (NIV)

You could find me with my siblings and neighborhood friends at the creek on most sunny and hot summer days. We would build a wall of rocks to make a little pool to splash around in to get relief from the heat. Many of our classmates who did not have the luxury of a self-made swimming hole had their own swimming pools or went to the public pool. Some even went on vacation to beat the summer heat.

We had the best swimming hole in the community, and we would get our share of summer exercise. Swimming is one of the best forms of exercise if you are looking to exercise all your muscles at the same time. Have you ever thought about the places where you enjoy going swimming? What is it about that place? Have you taken the necessary precautions when deciding when and where to go swimming? Safety and location are some of the things we consider before diving into the water. We would not consider swimming in an area that was not safe—unless you were a kid making a swimming hole in the neighborhood creek.

Why do we go to the unsafe swimming pool of past mistakes and regrets? Why do we dive or cannonball into a shallow pool that can pull you down like quicksand when we know the consequences? We want to go back and fix what broke in the wake of our cannonball. The longer we linger on those shores of past mistakes and regrets, the less stable the ground becomes. When we stand there, we are wasting time, and we are cheating ourselves of the peace and joy that come from serving God—and others—and spending time with Him.

Our time spent on those shores keeps us from spending time at the deep pool of God's love. We cannot recapture that time but we can decide to leave those unsafe shores. If we don't focus on God's love for us, we begin to doubt it. Don't! It is a tool of Satan to get us to forget God's wonderful salvation! We begin to doubt that God is bringing about good things for us even though we have made a poor choice. God is able to use all things—even lost time, regrets, and mistakes. Our time-warped minds will tell us to look at what we did and cause us to swim in dangerous pools. Think about the location of that pool and what it is filled with. God's pool is filled with love, mercy, joy, peace, and grace. He turned our swimming hole of muck, mire, and sin into an oasis!

Swimming in the pond, lake, or ocean of regret will only make us too tired to fulfill God's purpose for our lives. That is no way to worship God. He brought us out of the cesspool of sin and despair. Our energy and time need to be put to God's use! We need to let God use everything in our lives—even the bad stuff we did before we gave our souls to Jesus. God uses our despicable past (before repentance life) for our good and for His glory! God has put out the "No Swimming" sign. It is too dangerous!

Uneven Sidewalks

The steps of a *good* man are ordered by the Lord,
And He delights in his way.
Though he fall, he shall not be utterly cast down;
For the Lord upholds *him with* His hand.
—Psalm 37:23–24

"Step on the crack and break your mother's back." As children, we ambled down the sidewalk and tried our best to avoid stepping on the cracks. Some of those cracks were uneven, and if our toes got caught, stumbling was sure to follow.

Have you ever experienced a phantom trip when you were strolling? You stumble but haven't a clue about what grabbed the tip of your toe? Somehow you remain upright, look around for any potential embarrassment and continue on. I have had many phantom trips that I do not bother to look around anymore to see if anyone witnessed the sidewalk grabbing my toe. I have witnessed many others taking such trips. On one occasion I witnessed a mother holding her little boy's hand and answering her son's numerous questions. I watched intently as they were deep in conversation. She held his hand and kept him from falling on the uneven sidewalk. She held his complete attention in conversation, and they were so into each other that they were oblivious to everything else. If he had struggled to free himself from her gentle grasp, he might have fallen face first into the sidewalk and ended up with cuts and bruises.

God authorized all of our steps. When we are captivated or "into" Him, He has our hands. If we stumble or fall, He will keep us from being "cast down" or thrown against the pavement. He will keep us from being flung, thrown, or pitched into the things that would cause us to get scraped or bruised. We may fall, but we will not be dragged, lugged, yanked, or pulled recklessly to the ground when we trip and stumble because the Lord is the One who holds our hand. We will not experience total defeat and give up on trying to walk in this uneven world. He lifts us up higher. When we put one foot in front of the other, the uneven sidewalk does not control us—His hand does. We have joy in the Lord. He walks with us on our paths, holding us up and holding our hands. He keeps us from falling flat on our faces and feeling like failures.

Just as the mother took pleasure in watching her little boy bound down the sidewalk while totally trusting her and listening to her, the Lord takes pleasure in us. When we struggle to be free from His tender hand, the pleasure ends. We stumble and fall and our hearts end up with cuts and bruises. We feel totally defeated. Jesus will take our outstretched hands when we offer them to Him. He will lift us up and tend to our broken, shattered, and crushed hearts.

We no longer feel crushed or overpowered by the enemy. Jesus lovingly reminds us to never let go of His hand.

Helping hand

Conserve Energy

The Lord *is* my strength and my shield;
My heart trusted in Him, and I am helped;
Therefore my heart greatly rejoices,
And with my song I will praise Him.
—Psalm 28:7

"Turn off the lights. You're wasting energy." Have you ever heard these words? While growing up, the big energy-saving phrase was: "Close the door. We're not heating the outdoors."

We trust the seemingly never-ending supply of electric and heat for our homes and offices. If we did not trust the provider of these resources, we would spend all our time addressing these needs. Lacking trust is a tiring, draining, and exhausting way to live. Trusting that our own abilities will provide us with our needs is unwise and reckless.

We think we can have it all and do it all on our own. Our minds become tired and weary, and our strength begins to waver and fail. When we call on God and trust Him with our hearts, He helps us! God becomes our strength after we have depleted it. He becomes our trust after we have exhausted it. He becomes a shield of faith that will protect our minds and hearts from the recklessness that a lack of trust yields.

The shield of faith can be too heavy to carry on our own. The armor of God is quite heavy and requires a lot of energy to carry it, but we do not have to carry it alone. When we trust in Him the shield becomes weightless! We can have joy in the depths of our hearts! When the world tells us to trust the things in it—we have nothing but worry and dread. I'd rather conserve energy by carrying the shield of faith. Worrying squanders energy until there is nothing left. We are left empty.

Praising God for His goodness toward us is a good form of exercise. It gives us the energy for more praise. A heart leaping for joy is a positive form of using energy. Have you ever been drained and consumed by worry? Have you felt like you did not have enough strength left to face the day? That is a negative form of energy. Worrying robs us of joy and strength. It comes from a false sense of security of self and trying to go it alone.

We think, fret, and dwell upon the would'ves, could'ves, and should'ves when we try to make it on our own. That is wasted energy. We waste energy on things that cannot be changed. We become physically, emotionally, mentally, and spiritually worn. We are too tired to use our "trust-in-God" energy. Trust-in-God energy revives and refreshes our hearts and minds. When we use trust energy, we receive joy and strength and all we need from God.

We need to turn off the worry switch and give glory to God. Conserve energy now. The switch is at your fingertips. It is one call away. Jesus is not far away! The shield of faith is not as heavy as you think it is! Call out to Jesus! He hears our distress calls and rescues us from our worries and fears! He puts us in a safe place. He cares for us! Our joy comes from Him when we trust Him! Conserve energy and trust Jesus!

What Am I Forgetting?

Let all that I am praise the Lord; may I never forget the
good things he does for me.
—Psalm 103:2 (NLT)

"There is no need to complain because no one is going to listen." We hear this phrase quite often. After it has been stated, complaining typically follows. It is like they are giving a heads up to what the conversation is going to be. We are challenged to head in the opposite direction or steer the conversation toward an encouraging and uplifting topic.

Maybe we can be full of God's grace and listen to them as He listens to our complaining. If someone made a list of all that we are, would "complainer" be on the list or would "praiser of what the Lord has done for us" be in the top spot? There may be days when complaining seems to be the only option, but it is a thankless option. God only does purely good things for us that are for our benefit. God does not do bad things for us or things that are not beneficial to our total well-being.

Bad things may happen in our lives, but they are not from God. He created us with a free will and a free spirit that we misuse. Children can be raised by the godliest parents who taught them all about the love of God; a love that is not coerced. They have free will to choose whether to return that love to Him. If parents were to coerce their children, which is not biblical, into loving and obeying God, the free will they were created with is eliminated.

God did not create us with a coerced form of love. He created us with free will and love. We were made to be thankful and to praise Him. Have you ever thought about what the days were like in the Garden of Eden before Adam and Eve disobeyed God? They were free to praise and thank God for the benefits He gave them in the garden. They had uninhibited, spontaneous praise for God as He walked with them there. Nothing had broken the communion between them. They knew the sound of God as He walked in the garden when He came to be with them.

Being thankful for the simplest things and praising God with all they were was the norm. That was their relationship with God before Adam bit into the fruit that God had specifically instructed them not to have. Adam and Eve had only praises for God and enjoyed their communion with Him. That was "all that they were." All that they were, was all for God. However, they misused the free will God created them with. That is the origin of our complaining, our divisions, and the beginning of the grumbling in the world.

The "all that I am" includes our physical bodies, minds, hearts, and souls. Every aspect of our being affects our praise. If one of those is off, our praise will be too. When we are tempted to grumble about the forbidden fruit we don't have or about a situation that we have no influence over and we dwell on those things, we forget the One who gives us all things. We can praise God for all that we have: life, breath, legs, eyes, noses, hands, children, spouses, jobs, friends, and family. We praise Him for these things with all that we totally are.

Make a list of all the benefits you have today—and praise God for them with all that you are. Praising God for all the good things He does is an excellent memory exercise! I will praise God for everything that crosses my path today—good and bad!

Joyful

Until now you have asked nothing in my name. Ask, and
you will receive, that your joy may be full.
—John 16:24

Saying the word *joy* makes the face muscles almost automatically respond with an enthusiastic smile. One of my favorite words in the English language is joy! Just saying the word out loud triggers something deep down in the soul! Joy can trigger excitement when it has completely filled our hearts, minds, and souls or make us downcast and jealous when we see others have it when we do not.

It is difficult even to write the word *joy* without an exclamation point or in all caps! Joy is exclaiming! It exclaims that we have received something from God! It exclaims that we are thankful for what we have received from God. We cannot contain all the excitement of it! It exclaims that we desire for our lives what He desires for our lives!

Joy comes from believing and trusting that, when we ask, we will receive God's best for us. It may not always be what we expect. Does this mean we can ask for a new house, a new car, a new job, and well-behaved children and will receive it? When we ask for these things and other things that we believe we need or want—and do not ask God to look at them first to see if this is what He wants for us—we might miss out on joy's fullness and the peace from receiving what we asked for.

Satan would have us believe we have hit the joy mark since we are happy. We may think we are experiencing joy, but it is a false joy. Peace is masquerading as the one given by God. It is temporary in nature, and it will leave us asking and searching for that one true joy again and again in something else. We want the things we want. We think and believe they bring us joy. Maybe we ask for things without thinking about the repercussions on our lives or on the lives of others. Sometimes the things we ask for do not bring us the joy we thought they would. It may not be what God wanted for us. He may give it to us to experience that not everything we want is good for us or bring us pure joy.

Getting what we ask for when our asking comes from our desires and not what God desires is a hard lesson. Imagine a teen asking his or her parents if he or she can go to a party where alcohol will be present. The parent knows the possible outcomes and what is best for the teen. The parents do not want their son or daughter to go and let them know why. The teen continues to ask even though he or she knows that it is not what the parents want. The parents decide to give their son or daughter what they have asked for and allow the teen to go to the party. The son or daughter is injured in a severe car accident—and several of the child's friends do not survive. The joy from attending the "got-to-be-there" party was temporary. Unfortunately, that is the hardest of lessons.

Sometimes we encounter hard lessons, which are void of the joy we initially were seeking. We can ask for things without asking for them in His name—and we may get them with temporary happiness. When we ask God for things in His Name, we know, trust, and believe He will give them to us—and we will receive what is best for us. That is full and pure joy!

Left Hanging

I have been crucified with Christ and I no longer live, but
Christ lives in me. The life I now live in the body, I live by
faith in the Son of God, who loved me and gave himself
for me.
—Galatians 2:20 (NIV)

"I was born this way." "It's human nature." Have you heard these phrases before? Falling back on those phrases seems to say that Jesus is still hanging on that rugged, rough, heavy, sin-bearing cross waiting to die for the redemption of our sin nature. When we were born, we were unable to talk or walk. We were irresponsible for our actions, but we grew and matured. We learned to talk and walk and become responsible for ourselves. We did not remain immature. We grew up.

We have human nature, but continually relying on our humanness instead of the power of Jesus Christ is immature and irresponsible. Jesus died on the cross for our redemption of our "human nature". He liberated us from the sin nature and spirit we were born with and gives us the Spirit of God. We are a new creation!

We have either the spirit of human nature or the Spirit of Christ inside us. Think about that for a moment. Think about that when you want to blame others for your reactions to your circumstances. Think about how irresponsible it is to do that. Think before you act. Am I about to sin in my anger because someone is stepping on my rights or am I going to live by faith in the Son of God and trust that He has taken this human response and turned it into a responsible, Christ-like reaction?

Christ was crucified for our sin nature. Our sin nature died with Him, but that is not where it ends. His being raised from the dead by His Father is the most powerful event of all time. Why? That is where the transformation power begins. The power of overcoming sin and death comes from Christ. He died, but then He was raised into a new transformed body! If He were not raised from the dead, then there would be no point in following Him and wanting a "new life" to stop the choice to sin.

When we use human nature as an excuse, aren't we saying that "human nature" is greater than God's power to regenerate our hearts? Do we want a partial transformation from our old sinful selves? Are we using "human nature" as an excuse so we can keep on sinning? Do we rationalize our sinful actions, thoughts, and attitudes? Do we trust the power of the resurrection over sin and death? Do we trust a false form of grace that says that there is nothing we can do about human nature?

We ask Jesus to be Lord of our lives. We ask Him to come in, transform us, and we die to our human nature, and have Christ live in every part of us. We can live by faith that, with Him, we can live every day free from sin! Seek Him first, and it will be our desire to walk in that obedience. It will become our nature to make right choices and not rely on human nature to rationalize our bad ones.

We lay our sin nature down when we ask the Son of God to come and dwell with us. Maybe we have not "crucified" ourselves. Maybe our desires are not the desires of Christ Jesus. That is why we still say that the sin we do is human nature. Perhaps we are forgetting that we have been given a new, righteous, and resurrected nature. Have our hearts been transformed by the power of the living Christ or do they reveal that we have left Him hanging on the cross?

Holding onto rope

Sin Prevention

Your word I have treasured in my heart,
that I may not sin against You.
—Psalm 119:11 (NASB)

Even though my car had preventative measures—brakes—to keep me from hitting the car in front of me, I must have needed more practice to make them work properly. My lack of use or application of the preventative measure caused something bad to happen. Even though I was aware that my car had been properly equipped with brakes, I did not apply them this one particular time. Fortunately, there were no injuries.

All the preventions that are at our fingertips—fire and pest prevention, corrosion and accident prevention, and disease prevention that we spend much of our time, effort, and money on to prevent future damage to our homes, vehicles, and bodies—will not be beneficial if they are not put to use or practiced. We do not hesitate to spend time and money to call the exterminator to rid our houses of the creatures that eat away its core. We invest money on education for fire safety prevention and rust proofing our vehicles and education on auto and road safety. We invest millions of dollars in nutrition, exercise, disease-prevention remedies, and health education.

We treasure the things we have an invested interest in. Sin prevention seems to be a thing of the past. Has our invested interest in the prevention of it dwindled? What preventative measures are we equipping ourselves with? How much application do we have in using it to prevent sin from damaging our souls? What are we doing to prevent the damage to our futures? Do we have an invested interest in eternity? Do we put our effort and devotion in our desire to keep from sinning?

Treasure is putting into practice the preventative measure God has laid out for us to not sin. Our lives seem to be busy and full of preventative measures for our temporary yet seemingly important items, but when it comes to the eternal part of our lives, we sometimes look at it as something we do not have to invest a whole lot of prevention and practice into. We may have said the "hell-prevention prayer" for Jesus to save us from the sins we have already committed. However, we might not look to the future of how to prevent the sin from being committed again.

Having the preventative measure for sin is a great way to begin. But just as the brakes were in the car ready to be used, if we do apply them to keep us from hitting the car in front of us, they will not prevent an accident. We can own numerous Bibles, hear God's Word, and listen to many sermons or Bible studies, but until we consistently apply or treasure God's Word, we are likely to continue sinning against God.

We must treasure God's Word in our hearts and not our heads. Preventing sin without taking joy in the prevention or without our love for God, it then is a plain, joyless, unintentional, aimless way to live. There should be pure joy in treasuring God's Word—the prevention of sin. Treasuring God's Word in our hearts takes action. When we sin against God, we want to hide from Him. Our sins separate us from Him. Let us run to Him with repentance and acceptance of His great love for us!

Yes, We Can!

And when He had come into the house, His disciples
asked Him privately, "Why could we not cast it out?" So
He said to them, "This kind can come out by nothing but
prayer and fasting."
—Mark 9:28–29

Coaches, teachers, parents, and those who are in the training business
will say the word "can't" is not in their vocabulary. Defeat or rising
to the challenge are two ways we can react when we are faced with
situations that seem hopeless or overwhelming. Do we become defeated
as we focus on the situation? Do we rise to the challenge as we focus
on the one who gives us strength to face it? When we say, "I can't," we
are really saying, "I give up." We are saying, "It is all about me and not
about God."

We do not want to adjust our focus. Sometimes our focus is on
our own strength and perspective and not on God's strength and His
perspective. Our focus is on ourselves instead of God. We cannot
process death, a job loss, persecution, temptation, or any part of life
because we don't pray! We don't ask God to handle it for us because we
don't trust that He can.

What is our first reaction to horrific news of cancer, domestic
violence, or a close family or friend who is suffering from a horrible
addiction? We are shocked by what we hear and see. Almost immediately,
doubt, fear, and hopelessness become the focus. Have you ever thought
about what happens when you allow those initial emotions to linger?
It muddles up your focus, and a wave of defeat washes over you. Why
not rise to the challenge, pull up your bootstraps, and come with
boldness to God? Ask Him for strength and proper focus to face the
situation, and rely on Him to bring you through it. We waste time,
create mental anguish, and we create a blur when we don't get answers

to our questions. When we immediately take action with our hearts, souls, and minds by praying, we feel peace. The words of an old hymn by Scriven (1855) come to mind: "Oh what peace we often forfeit. Oh what needless pain we bear; all because we do not carry everything to God in prayer." ("What A Friend We Have in Jesus," n.p.)

We can pray, but praying and fasting together are powerful. We can focus our entire attention on God, move the situation from our spotlight, and allow God to become our focus. We can glorify God for all that He is. We can know through Him, all things are possible. We pray and fast until we see or hear the answer that God has provided.

We say we pray, but do we pray with our hearts, souls, minds, and strength? Is it the first thing we do? Do we want God to handle things? Do we pray with devotion, fervor, dedication, and affection? God has the power and authority to take care of things. He gives us the same power and authority when our hearts, souls, and minds are lined up with His.

We boldly follow Jesus and listen to His words and teachings, but we try to take care of things ourselves. Why don't we get it? Why don't we get the power of prayer and the power of fasting? Perhaps they are used too loosely or lightly and have caused them to lose much of their meaning and have become an actionless verb. Through prayer and fasting we can!

Today Is Today

This is the day the Lord has made;
we will rejoice and be glad in it.
—Psalm 118:24

Today is not tomorrow, yesterday, or someday. There is only one today. Today is unique. Your today is different from my today. No todays are the same. One today is all we get. We do not get more than one today at a time. Think about the today you have been given. Are you glad that you have today? If so, then rejoice. How can I rejoice with all the things I must face today?

Maybe we do not know about other people's todays, but God does. He made your today. It was made specifically for you—and not for anyone else. Since He knows your today, He commands us to rejoice. Grumbling and complaining about today means we are criticizing what God has made.

Adam and Eve began grumbling and criticizing after they sinned. Have you ever been inclined to grumble about your today? God makes every day—but not before it gets here. He has not made tomorrow yet. He does not make yesterdays. He does not make somedays. He makes today for us, today. We invented tomorrow, yesterday, and someday. Why are we so hung up on the tomorrows and yesterdays and somedays? Do we still have the forbidden fruit in hand? We cannot live yesterday, tomorrow, or someday, today. We have all that He wants us to have today.

When we are so wrapped up in tomorrow, yesterday, and someday, we are missing out on what He wants us to have today. If we look beyond today, we may find misery, anxiety, and strife. Jesus said, "Therefore do not worry about tomorrow, for tomorrow will worry about itself. Each day has enough trouble of its own" (Matthew 6:34 NIV).

God gives us all the blessings, strength, grace, and mercy we need for today. If He were to give us all the blessings, strength, grace, and mercy we need for the tomorrows, yesterdays, and somedays, we would not be able to handle all the wisdom, power, and glory. God is the only one who has that ability. He is infinite and sovereign. We are not.

What is the point of today? We must focus on God and rejoice in who He is. Rejoicing is a response to fully knowing who God is. The more we know God, the more rejoicing will take place—and there will be less grumbling and complaining. Tomorrow, yesterday, and someday are all about us. We have turned them into a god or idol and become obsessed. He commands us to rejoice in Him. Delight in Him. He is the true giver of joy, which causes us to rejoice and be glad.

We are reassured and thankful for today because He made it. He knows everything that today holds for us. He touched it with His loving, righteous hands before He gave it to us. We make a mess of our todays when we try to live yesterday, tomorrow, or someday today. What are you doing with the today He has made for you? Live today! Rejoice today! That is what He made it for!

Rehearsing

Therefore do not worry about tomorrow, for tomorrow will
worry about its own things.
Sufficient for the day *is* its own trouble.
—Matthew 6:34

Have you ever noticed that, no matter how many times you rehearse for a play, concert, wedding, or speech, it never goes exactly as it did during the rehearsal? Something is generally overlooked or forgotten during the rehearsal. Some of those things cannot be taken into consideration. Our minds are limited and cannot think of every scenario or possibility that could possibly take place. We use a lot of time in rehearsals to try to think of every scenario. We believe the events will be better if we rehearse more. We want the events to go just as we planned it—with no troubles or surprises. We want our tomorrows to go as we rehearsed them in our minds—with no surprises or troubles.

In this topsy-turvy world, we may feel like we are falling over the edge if life is not going the way we have rehearsed it in our minds. We speculate and rehearse our tomorrows. We add tomorrow's worries and trouble to the trouble we have today. Our minds become full of speculation about what could happen. We stop focusing on God. Our minds become absent of God.

We believe that the scenarios are real, creating trouble where there was none. As with most things, there is good and bad—and speculation is no exception. One can speculate with optimism or negativity. One will drag us into the pit of despair and desperation, causing our heart's focus to go awry. Doubt and fear dwell inside us. We will head down the road of denial. The other will cause us to look to God and trust that He has everything under control. He chooses to use us in our troubles to bring others to Him.

If we are constantly in speculation mode, we cannot live and face what is right before us. We miss out on opportunities to show others the love that God has for them. We miss out on giving and receiving the blessings He is ready to give to us. If we want fewer troubles, we need to stop rehearsing troubles that have not even arrived on our doorsteps. We only need to experience them once. Experiencing them more than once drains our energy.

Who wants to experience troubles more than once and live in a constant state of weariness? We seem to want that more often than not. Worry and fear about tomorrow's troubles stems from a lack of trust in God. He commands us to not fear.

Each day will have enough trouble. Why would we invite more trouble today? Why do we let tomorrow's troubles in the door? Bridges cannot be crossed until you are actually crossing them. A cart before the horse will not get you far. How can you worry about tomorrow before you have tomorrow? How do you even know what will take place tomorrow—or if tomorrow will even get here? You only multiply your troubles when you experience them over and over in your mind. Life is a reality show that cannot be rehearsed. Do not waste it with worries about tomorrow, which will only bring heaviness of spirit.

Hidden And Free

For in the time of trouble
He shall hide me in His pavilion;
In the secret place of His tabernacle
He shall hide me; He shall set me high upon a rock.
—Psalm 27:5

In *The Sound of Music,* the Von Trapp children are afraid of a thunderstorm. They run into their nanny's room, hoping their nanny will calm their fear of the storm. While trying to hide under their covers, they realize the storm still raged and they were still alone and afraid. The covers did nothing to relieve their fear. In the nanny's room, they sensed her love and felt protection from the storm. They broke out in a song about what to focus on when they were afraid or had troubles.

Trouble is a common word in this day and age. We all have trouble—some more than others. We often see others experiencing more trouble and wonder why that is. Many of our troubles come from our choices. We long to live free from chaos, stress, and trouble. We try to conceal or hide from our troubles with sleep, alcohol and drug use, business, or denial. After we have used up all that we have available at our fingertips, we still have the troubles. They still stare at us.

The trouble can seem worse after we try to escape it. We cannot remove trouble from our lives, and we cannot hide from it. We can be free while we are in our days of trouble. That sounds wonderful and almost too good to be true, but with God, *all* things are possible; not some things or things we can see how He is working but all things. God promises to "conceal me in His pavilion" "in the day of trouble."

God does not make promises that He does not keep. He keeps His promises. He is always faithful. The best hiding place from trouble is in His tabernacle. From His sanctuary, He watches us, protects us, and cares for us. Where is this tabernacle? Where is this sanctuary? It is where He is. That is called His presence. To be carefree in times of trouble, we must hide in His presence. He keeps our troubles in His care. He will hide us from our troubles when we are with Him. He becomes our sole focus, and our troubles fade into the background. We see His glory all around us.

Even though there may be trouble all around us, God lifts us up, leaving His glory in the wake. Even though the troubles may remain, He gives us a new perspective. We see Him before we look at the troubles in front of us. Trouble is never above us. We must meet and be with Him in His presence. We must seek God with our hearts, minds, souls, and strength. We must run into His sanctuary and let Him hide us under the covers of His protection until our troubles are past. That is where we find freedom from trouble. We are hidden and free. Are you seeking to dwell with Him in His sanctuary when troubles come?

Cliffhanger

The Sovereign Lord is my strength; he makes my feet like
the feet of a deer, he enables me to tread on the heights.
For the director of music; on my stringed instruments.
—Habakkuk 3:19

During deer-rutting season, I heard the rustling of leaves in the woods.
Then, in the silence I heard an eruption of noise and action as I witnessed
the chase during the rut. My heart raced as I sat and watched the two
bucks chasing a doe through the woods. Have you ever been witness to
deer running full-bore through dense woods? I was in awe and wonder
as three of God's creations ran through their natural habitat like they
were running in an open field. Nothing could stop them. How did they
move so quickly without going headlong into the trees? They moved
swiftly over the terrain, suddenly stopped, and went in the opposite
direction. The agility and strength of the deer was just breath taking.

Have you ever experienced weary feet that just want to stay put—
even if they were not in a safe place? Did the thought of moving them
through the deep woods of life seem like more work? God can make our
feet move like the deer through the deep woods in life. His strength in
us causes our joy and faith to increase. Imagine what pure confidence
in God—pure joy—looks like. Total trust and dependence on God will
turn our feet into deer feet. We run through life without crashing into
trees. We run without being out of control.

God gives us discipline and guidance as we walk, run, and climb
on the God-given pathway of life. He tells us to follow Him. He will
protect us, provide for all of our needs, and get us through the woods.
He is my strength. He will make me walk up high hills. My afflictions
are momentary. Are you out of the woods yet? What are you chasing?
Don't crash into the trees. Does your pathway look like it is filled with
rocks, briars, woods, and thistles? Does it even look like a pathway?

If we learn to trust God and accept the trials, troubles, briars, and mountains of stone along this path, He will give us blessings, pure joy, and increased faith. That is better than anything our little minds can fathom. We will be in awe as He sets our feet on the heights above what we know. We can trudge or run recklessly through the briars, get cut, stumble on the rocks, crash into the trees, bruise our bodies, and curse God for them or do we give our hands to Him to hold? Do we trust Him to walk us through the woods, up the path, past the briars, and over the rocks?

Take Jesus' hand and walk the path He has planned for you. His strength will flow through you, and He will enable you to walk through the briars and over the stony mountain. Grow closer to Him, lean on Him more, and love Him more. As I give Him my hand, I look into His loving eyes and say, "Oh, what joy!"

Seeing Wind

> But when he saw that the wind *was* boisterous, he was
> afraid; and beginning to sink he cried out, saying,
> "Lord, save me!"
> —Matthew 14:30

Have you ever seen the wind? Clouds swirling, dust devils twirling, leaves blowing, pine branches whispering, flags waving, and waves on top of the water are some of the effects we notice. Some winds help move us along like we are in a sailboat. Without it, we would not reach the other side of the lake. Wind is necessary to operate some power equipment. Threatening winds instill fear in us. What would our responses be if we could see the actual wind and not just the effects of it?

Have you ever considered how winds can bring about life-ending or life-altering events? What is our response to those types of winds? We can continue to look at those winds with fear or call on the one who will say, "Peace be still."

Peter did not appear to be afraid of the wind while he was in his boat. He was not afraid of the wind when he was obeying Jesus and getting out of the boat. He did not give Jesus any excuses for why he should not get out of his boat. He obeyed Jesus. What caused Peter to begin to sink? Peter saw wind. He saw the thing that caused his fear. He saw his fear instead of keeping his eyes on Jesus. Jesus erases fear with His perfect love.

Peter took his eyes off of Jesus for a split second and looked at the violent wind that could have easily taken his life. What caused Peter to take his eyes off of Jesus? What causes us to take our eyes off of Jesus? In a split second, our hearts can sink with despair. I wonder if Jesus showed Peter the wind so Peter would see how powerful He is and how weak Peter was. We cannot calm the wind or solve all the problems and trials that come our way. We do not have to succumb to the fear that problems or trials bring as they can crash over us like rushing waves. We can trust that Jesus will not let us sink beneath the waves. He pulls us up when we call out to Him to save us. He causes the wind to blow. He commands it to stop with His presence or His words.

Have you ever seen enough wind to cause you to fear? I have not. I've heard reporters ask people who have seen the mighty winds. They say, "I cried to God for safety. I cried to God to get us through and keep us safe." Maybe that was the kind of wind Peter saw. It gives us no choice but to cry out to God to save us. He is right there.

Peter saw Jesus, and he saw the wind. When Jesus and Peter were in the boat together, the wind stopped. We may look at the wind around us even when Jesus is right in front of us. When we let Jesus into our boats, the fear-causing wind will subside. He will rescue us from the wind. When we do not let Him in our boats, we focus on the wind.

Let Jesus in your boat—and watch what happens to the wind.

20/20 Vision

Now He who has prepared us for this very thing *is* God,
who also has given us the Spirit as a guarantee. So *we are*
always confident, knowing that while we are at home in
the body we are absent from the Lord. For we walk by
faith, not by sight.
—2 Corinthians 5:5–7

We do not see a paycheck before we invest any time on the job, but we have enough faith to go to work. We do not see the fish in the lake, stream, or ocean, but we throw our lines into the water in hopes of catching fish. If we wait to see a paycheck without working for it, we will never see it. If we wait to see the fish before we set out to catch them, we will never see the fish on the end of our line.

We have enough faith to know that we will receive pay if we work and we might catch a fish if we go to the lake. Our faith in these things influences our actions and expectations of searching for what is before us. Imagine people not having the faith to know that something is waiting for them at the end of the workweek or at the end of the fishing line. The things we do not see but hope for play a big part in our actions as we seek to obtain them.

God is not visible to our eyes, but that does not mean He is less than the things we do see. In fact, He is more than all that is seen or unseen. It also does not mean that striving to be close to Him or give testimony of His love for us is unfitting or inappropriate. God's purpose for us is to spend our lives with Him—now and forever.

Consider your actions. What are they saying about your faith in God? Even though we cannot see God, He gave us His Spirit as a promise that He is striving with us in our faith—even when there are sufferings, broken hearts, or broken dreams. Even when we cannot see

Him, He is with us! We can be courageous, fearless, and bold—even when we cannot see God or feel Him near.

It would be easy to walk away from God and toward something we can see and that we think will alleviate the pain and suffering. That only brings more pain and more suffering. When we walk away from God, we separate ourselves from the loving-kindness of His heart. We convince ourselves that we do not need anyone. We have false dependence on ourselves. We are lonely. Our minds and hearts cannot see others around us. We do not see their needs or see them as Jesus sees them.

Walking in faith, we love more than if we walk by sight. Sight is of ourselves, and faith is of the Spirit of God. He is love. When we walk the path of life with faith in Jesus, we have His sight. His sight is clearer than anything our human eyes can see. Even with this clearer sight, our feet may stumble. We may fall or fail. We may need Jesus to carry us, but our faith-vision will become even more natural and more constant. We will grow closer to Him and feel His heartbeat. We will become more dependent upon His love. He longs for us to accept perfect vision, and we long to receive it!

Faithfulness Attraction

The Lord's lovingkindnesses indeed never cease, For His
compassions never fail. They are new every morning;
great is Your faithfulness.
—Lamentations 3:22–23 (NASB)

We hear many empty promises from candidates for elected offices.
Sometimes they are made to get people to like them and vote for them.
Sometimes parents, bosses, and others in leadership positions make
promises to be liked or popular or to avoid arguments. Some promises
are made with good intentions but without the loving kindness of the
Lord.

Our intentions may fall by the wayside. We may promise to be
there for a baseball game, piano recital, or wedding—only to let the
other person down. Think of the times you have been let down because
someone did not follow through on a promise. Unmet expectations
also let us down. Is it possible that you believed they were unloving or
unkind? Did anger and bitterness set in? Consider a time when you were
not able to keep your promise and let someone down.

Promises are broken frequently. It comes from a heart of selfishness.
In the minutes, hours, and weeks after 9/11, we became a loving and
kind community. We were willing to be there for others. We saw
compassion, goodwill, and unselfishness. We heard amazing stories of
loving kindness and kept promises.

We are still amazed when we hear reports of loving and kind deeds
done for others, especially when they are undeserved. That is how God
is toward us. We are undeserving of His loving-kindness. We neglect
Him, turn away from Him, and refuse to do His will for our lives.
Most people are attracted to kind, compassionate, and loving people.
We seldom observe people running to be close to those who are unkind,
unloving, or uncompassionate.

Have you ever stopped to consider what attracted you to the love of Jesus? Those who follow Jesus closely take on His characteristics of compassion, loving-kindness, and faithfulness. They attract those who seek changes in their lives and those who want to walk with Jesus. Maybe that is why He had such a crowd around Him and why it was necessary for Him to go off alone to be with His Father. He wanted to remain compassionate, loving, kind, and faithful to His Father and others.

The pure love and kindness of God are renewed every day. His flawless love and kindness should flow through our flawed person. We have been made flawless by the blood of Jesus—and that should be attractive to others. Sometimes we are not. We may perceive our kindness as flawless but our hearts may not be on the love and kindness page of faithfulness to God. That page includes sacrificing our wants and our agendas.

We can be callous, merciless, vindictive, and malicious because we do not go off alone to be with God and allow Him to transform us with His powerful love. We do not like to be around those who only have their own interests at heart. They do not want to be around us if that is how we conduct our lives.

Faithfulness to God comes from loving Him with all our hearts, souls, minds, and strength. We set aside our wants and our agendas for His. Love will flow from our hearts, hands, and feet to those we travel with every day. How do we know God's love is flowing through us? How do we know it is attractive? If we are faithful to God in every area of our lives, His loving-kindness will show in us. Does your compassion and loving-kindness attract others to Jesus? Do people see the faithfulness of God through your compassion and loving-kindness?

Crown Wearers

For the sun rises with a scorching wind and withers
the grass; and its flower falls off and the beauty of its
appearance is destroyed; so too the rich man in the midst
of his pursuits will fade away. Blessed is a man who
perseveres under trial; for once he has been approved, he
will receive the crown of life which the Lord has promised
to those who love Him.
—James 1:11–12 (NASB)

Once upon a time, there was a land with acres of lush green lawns that surrounded a rich king's estate. The gardens were full of colorful blooms, climbing vines, stone garden paths, statues and sculptures, and benches to captivate all the senses. Keeping the estate in such beautiful splendor required hours of paid labor (since the king did not permit royalty to go work), gallons of water, and fertilizer. The king supplied everything because he had great power and wealth.

One day, the sun rose with such a searing heat that all the lush gardens and lawns dried up. They became brown, crunchy, and brittle. Despite all of the king's endeavors, he could not bring the once most magnificent estate back to its former glory.

In the village, the lowly people worked their minuscule pieces of land that were full of rocks, stumps, thistles, and briars. They toiled diligently to try to bring forth food to feed their families. They persevered day in and day out as they worked out in their fields. They praised God they had land to work and families to feed. They trusted God and had faith in Him to provide for them despite all the hardships they faced. They knew the ground would bring forth what was necessary for them to live.

The king could not believe it when he heard them being joyful in their toiling. He became jealous of their joyfulness and devised a plan to have one of the villagers brought to his castle to dismantle his joy.

The humble villager was afraid of what the king might do. He cried out to God to go with him. The king tried to rob the villager of his joy by trying to get him to believe he was a nice king who wanted to help them. He had a table that was filled with all kinds of delectable food. The villager had never seen anything like it.

The king offered him the best guest quarters in the castle and a second seat to his throne. When the king believed he had the villager in his grip, he asked how he had joy despite his destitute state.

The villager began to share a story of love from the Bible. Before he could complete it, the king announced that he had heard enough—and he sent the villager to the dungeon. The king had many enemies chained in the dark, damp, dreary, and varmint-infested dungeon. In spite of all that was happening to them, they praised God for His love and for each other. They were not alone, and they broke out with a song of joy glorifying the King of Kings! They sang so loudly that the king could no longer endure keeping them in his dungeon. He ordered one of his men to release them and send them away.

The king's men were so enthralled by the joy of the villagers that they decided to go with them. They left the castle and began trusting God to provide for them.

The king was left alone in an empty, dreary castle, and the humble villagers received victory, blessings, and the crown of life. The glorious crown does not rust. It is the ultimate reward of grace for a life lived for the Lord!

Reference

Scriven, J. M. (1855). What a friend we have in Jesus. Retrieved from http://www.cyberhymnal.org/
  htm/w/a/f/wafwhij.htm

About the Author

Carol Jimerson is a wife, mother of three adult children and grandmother of two delightful boys. She is a United States Postal Service city letter carrier in her hometown of Corning, New York and loves giving smiles while interacting with her business customers. She has recently graduated from Ohio Christian University with a degree in Leadership and Ministry. She began her devotional writing on her blog www.coffeeonmydeck.blogspot.com. She has been published in Light From The Word a Wesleyan Publishing House devotional. She is also pursuing writing her Jonah story that she hopes will encourage others to share their story to uplift and encourage all of their need for Jesus. She receives her inspiring thoughts and words from God as she can be found out in His creation as much as possible, even when she is off the work clock, in her vegetable garden or walking through the woods with her camera in hand.

Printed in the United States
By Bookmasters